HOW TO IMPROVE AUSTRALIA'S DEMOCRACY

Breaking the Vicious Cycle!

Klaas Woldring

Typeset by BookPOD

Cover artwork © Klaas Woldring

ISBN: 978-1-922270-41-2 (pbk)
ISBN: 978-1-922270-37-5 (ebook)

Dedicated to Aafke

Other publications from the author:

Woldring, K. (2018) - *YES, we can ....rewrite the Australian Constitution*, BookPod/Amazon.

Woldring, K. & others (2015) - *Beyond Federation – Options to renew Australia's 1901 Constitution*, BookPod/Amazon, (Man. Editor)

Woldring, K. (2013) - *Australia Reconstructed*, BookPod/Amazon.

Woldring, K. (2006) – *How about OUR Republic?* BookSurge, (ISBN 1-4196-3175-6)

Woldring, K. (2005) – *AUSTRALIA Republic of US Colony?* Lulu POD, 329 pp. (ISBN 1-4116--4926-5)

Woldring, K. (1996), *Business Ethics in Australia and New Zealand in the Private and Public Sectors* - Essays and Cases, Melbourne: Nelson ITP (Initiated the book, wrote Introduction, one Chapter, Conclusion, and three linking statements, plus sole editorship), 23 readings and 12 cases, pp. 310 (ISBN 0 17 009113 9)

Woldring, K. (1984), Sole editorship. Introduction, conclusion and **three** chapters in *Beyond Political Independence - Zambia's Development Predicament in the 1980s*, Berlin: Mouton. Initiated the book and responsible for approximately 65% of it (hard cover), pp. 250 (ISBN 3-11-009951-9)

Woldring, K. and Gallagher, J. (1979), *The Impact of the Northern Rivers College of Advanced Education on the Far North Coast of New South Wales - Political and Cultural Aspects*, Lismore: NRCAE publication

CONTENTS

INTRODUCTION

The Covid-19 virus has shaken up Australia and the world. In part, that could turn out to be an unexpected bonus. Not that the mindset has suddenly turned to issues of governance, the systems that have been handed down to Australia from the Westminster heritage, the colonial period and the admired US example of federation. Temporarily in any case, the focus is elsewhere, understandably. In mid-April 2020 an IPSOS report about priority issues resulting from the health shock provided the following result:

> Healthcare 55%, Economy 47%, Unemployment 39%, Environment 22%, Cost of Living 22%. In January 2020, following the extensive bushfires and drought, the state of the environment topped the list with a record 41%.

Nevertheless, the disenchantment with the political system in Australia, especially the combative, adversarial attitude of the major parties in parliaments, has reduced the trust in politicians and the system probably as never before. When the worst of the Coronavirus threat is over Australia will still be left with the same governance systems of yesteryear in which the trust of the voters has declined seriously. The recent book by former PM Malcolm Turnbull, published as the worst of the health crisis seemed to ease off, yields plenty of reminders of the deep-seated governance system weaknesses. Turnbull, who was widely regarded as a promising PM for and by middle Australia, was bundled out by the right-wing faction of his own party. In large part he was a casualty of the system. The fundamentals of these unsatisfactory structures, understandably, are likely to return after the crisis and call for alternatives to be developed. The time has come to consider such alternatives and look ahead; and to break the vicious cycle.

Already the quick, unexpected creation of the National Cabinet, formed to deal with the crisis, is a remarkable development that provides more than a glimmer of hope. The Cabinet has indeed presented ways of tackling issues of huge national importance. This has not been experienced since the Great Depression, with the exception perhaps of the outbreak of World War II. It reveals an underlying preparedness by the major parties, to at least cooperate for this particular purpose. What could this mean for the future? Could it extend to consideration of alternative governance systems and possibly other breakthroughs? The paucity of such alternative suggestions in Australia is quite concerning. There may be some good reasons for that conservatism, but the arguments for major changes now are more compelling than ever. We will look at them in this text. It may also indicate a preparedness of politicians to organise public inquiries towards that end; and, especially, by the generally conservative media to provide avenues for discussion of alternatives. With some exceptions, referred to in this text, there has been little evidence of that. However, above all we need bold action rather than lengthy inquiries and Royal Commissions. This text is primarily action oriented. It favours the Carpe Diem principle.

Many Australians have not had the benefit of serious *comparative* political education. They also live quite far away from countries with different systems, except New Zealand, where since 1996 a new electoral system has had very positive effects. Australian educational systems have failed in this respect. Even the universities do not provide a great deal of in-depth study about *alternative* systems. The Westminster heritage dominates the intellectual debate. There is a good deal of basic instruction about the existing and perhaps other systems in English-speaking countries but that is actually in itself quite limiting. In contrast, European systems have to offer more for this purpose but very little is taught about them. As a migrant from the Netherlands who has lived and taught in several countries, I offer a series of different perspectives.

It is altogether a discussion primarily based on common sense.

The Australian universities have gradually, but effectively, been commercialised by making their existence – and growth – increasingly dependent on the fees of thousands of foreign, mostly Asian students. No less than one third of Australia's export income derives from their fees!

Universities are educational institutions, not commercial enterprises. We could see this new form of privatisation coming in the early nineties. Many academics have expressed serious reservations about this trend even though the advantages of such contacts with Asian countries are undoubtedly important for Australia's long-term future.

The teaching of Australian politics has actually suffered considerably in this process. Of course, it was and is not a primary interest of foreign students. Democracy has suffered in this period. The silence of Australian students in this period is a reflection of the trend. In the 1970s and 1980s that was quite a different story. The influence of foreign students today, especially Chinese students, has resulted in Universities tending to restrict expressing controversial ideas essentially because they have become dependent on their income. This trend does not favour free expression and democracy values.

In addition, few Australian political scientists are involved in seeking explanations for the current system malaise; even fewer who have considered major alternatives to the status quo. As a retired Associate Professor, with a Ph. D. in Political Science of UNSW, I have written about possible alternatives in books, web magazines and done podcasts for the last 15 years. There are remedies and, while the number of tenured academic staff has declined considerably, those who have tenure should speak up. This is a major benefit that comes with tenure. Regrettably, they seem to be very much part of the political conservatism that has prevailed for far too long. Why is this so? The short answer seems to be that there is a cultural bias in favour of the existing system amongst academics, and consequently also among their students, including journalists and editors, who shy away from venturing outside the square. Also, those who do favour major changes seem to have given up as the task appears to be "too difficult". Another answer may be that the current phase of dissatisfaction is seen as a temporary hiccup, a derailment that somehow will fix itself because "basically the system is satisfactory". Economic progress in the last 30 years has been reasonably good for most people even though inequality of income in Australian society has undoubtedly grown significantly. At the time of writing, understandably, the pandemic issue and recovery of the economy have priority. How is the cost of this period and the economic recovery going to be dealt with? But there remain major governance system issues that are at least equally important, even more important in the longer term, which cannot, at least should not be swept under the carpet. No, the system is no longer "satisfactory". And even if some services are satisfactory Australia can really do a lot better. When the country gets over the shock of the pandemic that will even be more essential. Our democracy is under serious threat. In addition, the competence of our federal government, is widely questioned. The quality of their environmental policies, specifically, is seen as seriously inadequate.

The major parties' leaders themselves have not shown much inclination to tackle the governance system issues, to the contrary. The politicians' complacency in this regard has emerged as a problem in itself. Although still sketchy they seem to concentrate essentially on adjusting the economy to rapidly changing external circumstances. This suggests at least an inclination, possibly even a preference to move away from nasty, adversarial debates. Nevertheless, there is in fact much more room for political system improvement. This short text aims to highlight these problems and suggest remedies. It questions the suitability of several existing systems. These may have served their purpose in the past, but they have now become a hindrance to good government. The general public and more especially the young are asking these questions increasingly. Frequent reference is made nowadays to the "old parties" and not just by the Greens. "Old" is of course not always dysfunctional and some of the systems may remain useful, but it'll be a matter of fitting those parts into a new constitutional, electoral and governance set of systems. It is a tall order to effect major change, but it can be done.

Cultural system bias occurs as a result of growing up and studying in a particular culture. That phenomenon is only natural of course but unless there is exposure to other cultures, for some time preferably, the belief develops that one's own culture, ways of doing and seeing things and solving problems, is regarded as more or less the only way or often even the best way. Xenophobia, fear of foreigners and systems foreign, may develop. Solutions to social, political and economic problems suggested by foreigners or foreign examples will simply not be understood and/ or distrusted. Still, in many ways Australia has developed as a reasonably successful multicultural society; that must be a positive basis. However, at the executive and elite levels, multicultural representation and acceptance of non-Anglo governance systems and values have lagged behind.

Political scientists mostly engage in study projects that are part of their own Australian culture, problems that are occurring within their familiar system, the federal/Westminster hybrid. The electoral system also was largely inherited and adapted from the UK's single member-district system. Even the addition of the Hare-Clark system of proportional representation introduced in Tasmania early in the 20th century, much later in the Senate and ACT, was an adaptation of British models (Thomas Hare); even though not actually used there. The Anglosphere creates opportunities for scholars and others to get exposure to and in other English-speaking countries. However, few explored beyond this language barrier partly because instruction in other languages is fairly rudimentary in Australia. Nevertheless, with English it is of course possible to gain experiences in other language countries. A small number of Australian political scientists have gained such experiences, generally to their advantage.

The influx of large numbers of migrants and refugees post WWII has nevertheless contributed much to diversification of the Australian society. In many spheres Australian society has been enriched further by adopting styles and systems from outside the Anglo sphere. In architecture Danish and Italian ideas were adopted. In all branches of the arts Australia was quite ready, eager even, to branch out. The variety in food preparation and presentation exploded through international influences. In the sciences Australia is in the forefront of innovation. In Medical Science and Vet Science Australia ranks highly and is constantly in touch with major developments elsewhere. Its educational systems match the best in the world, despite a decline in some tertiary institutions. In other words, other cultures in these branches of activity are NOT restricted. Why then has innovation in governance systems lagged behind so seriously?

During my 27 years teaching and researching in Australian universities I have found that, among academics and political journalists, the knowledge of other political and electoral systems is limited; and strongly coloured by the political culture they grew up with. That includes Republican systems as became clear during the Republic debate in the 1990s. The view of Republican systems was generally fairly negative, in spite of the major ally, the powerful USA, having a Republican system; and in spite of there being many other positive examples of Republics! Australians are somewhat better informed on the subject-areas of international relations and foreign policies than, say, comparative politics or comparative constitutional examples. Of course, again, there are notable exceptions.

But when it comes to governance system problem solving and real reforms this is left to the politicians and their advisers. Only a minority of them have much idea of foreign systems often despite traveling quite extensively in the world. In the last few years Australia's parliamentary politics and party membership have shown to be in deep trouble, resulting in very low membership numbers, but hardly any innovative solutions have been advanced for reform. Those who made attempts have soon given up because they were not published or listened to. Furthermore, the major party straight-jackets don't suit innovators and innovations. Problem solving tends to first-of-all be attempted in the traditional way, *within the existing system by means of piecemeal tinkering.* Moving outside the square is generally avoided, resented or just not understood. E.g., the number of people who do not grasp the practices of proportional representation – party list is staggering. That includes many academics, politicians and journalists. Drawbacks of the Westminster system are rarely mentioned, as for instance the need for Ministers to be "in and of the Parliament". This seriously limits the competence of Federal and State Governments! The Westminster dominance of the Government and Opposition in the legislatures, often serves no useful function other than theatrical performances of a usually hostile, adversarial, combative and unproductive nature. All these things are rarely questioned as a system flaw *to be addressed.* How much further and longer must the Parliament struggle for that to happen? The time has come to question this deep system conservatism in BOTH major parties and in the Trade Union movement as well.

In June 2020 a remarkable uprising happened in the United States when an African American George Floyd, a protester against the policies of the Trump Administration, was killed by police. A policeman kept his knee on his neck; Floyd protested and called out that "he could not breathe" but the policeman persisted with his behaviour and the protester died as a result. Widespread protest marches followed and, equally remarkably, similar protests sprang up immediately after the event in Australia as well.

The Australian public were reminded that several similar incidents had happened in Australia and that, in fact, 432 Indigenous citizens had died in Australian prisons since 1991 without there being any prison warder or policeman having been held responsible for this. What were the causes? Australians were also reminded that a Royal Commission of 1991 had made several recommendations to improve the situation but that most of these recommendations had not been followed up. The explosion of anger about Australian racism followed a similar pattern to that in the United States. Widespread protests were held in many Australian cities during the weekend of June 5th – 7th despite the still severe restrictions in place about public meetings in connection with the Coronavirus pandemic.

Soon, further protest action was advocated in Australia against statues and monuments reminding people of the colonial past, in the UK, South Africa and the US. PM Scott Morrison, who earlier had wanted to spend $50 m. on the renewal of the damaged statue of James Cook in Sydney, declared that Australia "had never known slavery". May be not quite like in the U. S. but similarities in treatment exist. The media literally exploded with several major articles by historians and other critics that this was a deficient reading of history. Mr. Morrison apologised for his comments but Australians were again puzzled by the PM's lack of well-known facts of Australian colonial history.

Suddenly, although the pandemic crisis had been handled initially well with a low dead figure of 102 by mid-June, Australia found itself involved in a further crisis. Researchers in Melbourne found that three out of four Australians were in fact "racist". Really, whatever that means exactly, there is still a huge underlying issue to be solved here as well.

Undoubtedly, the message that 432 Indigenous people have died in prison since 1991 came as a very unpleasant surprise to many Australians. Apart from three or four high profile shocking mistreatments of Indigenous youths, for instance the display of obnoxious and racist behaviour by prison wardens in Darwin, publicity has been minimal and inadequate. Nevertheless, the responses by the political system have also been inadequate over a long period of time. The protests by the Indigenous people and a large number of sympathetic non-Indigenous people brought this reality into sharp focus.

Therefore, the inadequacy of Government in relation to the Indigenous people, and of one leading mining corporation as well, is a reality. In this text the consequences of that reality are discussed. It is a package of consequences, quite apart from the federal structure, the complexity and inadequacy of which is of a different order than the colonial Westminster heritage. Moreover, we have a Government now that does not understand the priority of acting effectively on climate change. Australia does NOT need more Inquiries and recommendations by Royal Commissions. We need action now. We need major changes. First of all, we need different people in Government, something that can be achieved via changes to the electoral system. Furthermore, ministerial positions can be filled by people who are not elected as is the practice in many other democracies. Conservatism has nothing to offer here. Clearly, there is also much more to be done than "creating more jobs".

However, politically Australia is caught in a vicious circle, one which continues after every election or even after every new Prime Minister. This vicious circle is continued largely as a result of the electoral system which produces two major parties in the lower house of the Parliaments. Each of these parties comprise two major factions, the more numerous of which is the de facto Government. Thus, the current Coalition Government is dominated by its Right-Wing faction while, when the ALP is in power, the Government is dominated by their Right-Wing faction. The only way to break this vicious circle is to change the electoral system which produces this situation. Proportional Representation – Party List results in a *majority*

Coalition. This reform would have to be the very first step in breaking the vicious circle of Australian politics.

Any plan or proposals for major governance overhaul need not only to consider the important aspects to be tackled but also provide a logical and manageable order to do so; and explain why. A huge stumbling block has proved to be the colonial Constitution itself but to achieve constitutional changes the two-party system has been THE major stumbling block. Therefore, electoral system change must have high priority. **Fortunately, this is achievable without constitutional reform**. The principal reason for that is that the existing Constitution of 1901 has left the decisions about electoral systems very clearly to be decided by the Parliaments of the Federation. Some commentators have questioned this view, but a detailed examination suggests that it is correct. We should also mention the introduction of proportional representation (Hare-Clark) for the Senate by the ALP in 1948, just prior to the 1949 federal election. If that had been unconstitutional it would have been opposed on that ground, but it wasn't. PR was actually supported then even by "many conservative party leaders joining the ranks of parliamentary reform: such as Cook, Page, Bruce, McEwen and Menzies", wrote political scientist John Uhr in an excellent background piece (in *Representation and Institutional Change,* 1999).

That article also provides a very nuanced consideration of support for proportional representation before and after Federation in 1901 until 1948. There was fluctuating support by the major parties for the Senate subsequently, largely resulting from the difficult combination of having the two houses of the federal parliament elected by different electoral systems. The obvious solution to this problem is to now extend the proportional system to the House of Representatives – but on the basis of Party List, not Hare-Clark. This would end the two-party dominance and improve the democratic values and character significantly. It would introduce a new political culture which requires cooperation between parties rather than adversarial interaction. From that position it can only become easier to consider and implement further governance system reform.

At the end of May, 2020 a number of remarkable and unexpected first steps to initiate governance system change had in fact been taken by the Morrison government. The National Cabinet, put together to deal with the onset of the Coronavirus, would continue and replace the Council of Australian Governments (known as COAG). The PM was quoted as saying that "the National Cabinet would be driven by a 'singular agenda' which would be to 'create more jobs'. Leaders will meet each fortnight going forward and will eventually transition to monthly meetings once the pandemic is over." State leaders remained at odds over whether to reopen borders, but PM Scott Morrison was of the view that 'this won't be a barrier to a Trans-Tasman travel bubble".

Secondly, the PM said that he is "looking for an end to adversarialism". That sentiment goes actually well beyond solving complexities to be resolved by newly established five work groups to tackle them. Adversarialism is the ingrained, costly political culture of Australia, in the legislatures and in industrial relations. It would very likely be highly productive to end it. To do that requires governance system change. In industrial relations this means introducing workplace democratic programs, as operated in many European countries, as well as effective employee share ownership. Reformers can go back to the ground-breaking ACTU/TDC report of 1987, recommending European models. That was rejected then because "it is not our culture", according to the popular Bob Hawke. However, the adversarial culture seems clearly on the nose now, an unexpected COVID-19 bonus. Australians should widen the conversation and consider the alternatives that certainly available.

This book does not deal with the undoubtedly important Climate Change issue and the thus far inadequate approaches to that pressing problem by the Morrison government. It certainly is most surprising that the current Government does not accept the views of several senior environmental scientists in Australia urging it to act. One can only hope that the decision to tackle the Coronavirus crisis head-on, based on scientific medical advice, will provide the appropriate example to follow for climate change policies in the near future. Coal is no longer supported as a sound energy producer. The escape to promoting hydrogen now, instead of renewable energies, is not a sound solution at all either. We need decision-makers in Canberra who understand that. The political system needs to be changed to achieve that. Our democracy has to be improved and strengthened. The majority of the people, the majority of major corporations and financial institutions, support the rapid development of renewal energies of which there is an abundance available in Australia. Democracy means Government by the People, in practice by their elected representatives. These are not in power in Canberra today. That has to change.

CHAPTER 1

CONSERVATISM HAS DOMINATED THE ENTIRE POLITICAL SYSTEM SINCE FEDERATION

When the author Thomas Keneally began his campaign for an Australian Republic in 1990, now already 30 years ago, he began by pointing out to the Australian people that apart from appointing an Australian President as Head of State "nothing else would change". He said that because he believed that most Anglo-Australians would be hesitant to separate the government and the society in some way from the British Monarchy. And then, he added, it would be a Republic that still remained a member of the Commonwealth headed by that British Monarch. A very cautious approach. In the period before the Referendum – after a crash course by the Government and other organisations in Australian Politics and Republics to bring the many uninformed up to speed – the Referendum question was doctored by the Convention, comprising half selected citizens and half politicians, to suit the politicians. The President would be a symbolic politicians' President, chosen by two thirds of the federal parliament, not a directly elected President by the people. However, sixteen percent of the voters opposed that proposal solely or largely because they did not want a politicians' President. Instead they wanted a symbolic one, with a role similar to that of the Governor-General, who was elected directly by the people. As a result, it failed even though, as ALP leader Kim Beazley had warned, it could be another 20 years before there would be another such opportunity. Sadly, he even proved to be over-optimistic! This goes to show just how conservative particularly the major parties were then, actually more so than the voters at the time. The sixteen percent were most likely all pro-Republic voters! The major parties have not revisited the Republic issue since until quite recently. The issue was revived briefly when Malcolm Turnbull became PM in 2015 but that did not result in a new Referendum. The general disenchantment with politicians and the system would seem to suggest that the people may now regard other aspects of the system as more in need of reform and renewal. In particular, the federation is seen by many as a strange way to carve up the continent. More are making suggestions for regional divisions of a different kind. The definition of region can have many meanings. Some argue that the availability of rivers and water generally should determine what regional boundaries should be. More about that when we look at the problems of federation.

Since the 1977 constitutional referendum (discussed later) no changes have been made to the Constitution. Effectively, governments gave up entirely after a group of four referendum proposals failed in 1988. To his credit, with the 1977 referendum PM Fraser managed to put a stop to the abuse of an important constitutional convention. The replacement of two resigning Senators by others who did not represent the same party was regulated by an approved constitutional amendment to Section 15 regarding the replacement of casual vacancies. This abuse by the then Premiers of NSW and Queensland had played a major role during the sacking of Prime Minister Gough Whitlam in 1975. Amazingly, quite puzzling really, it was the first time that political parties were mentioned in the archaic Australian Constitution. On the next occasion, in 1988, when after two years of serious preparation by a team of highly qualified members, four modest reform amendments were placed before the voters, all four were rejected. The Liberal/NP Party Coalition rejected them. It became clear that unless both major parties wholeheartedly support a constitutional amendment, there is no hope to update the Constitution whatsoever. The conservative forces in the Coalition prevailed. They dominate the Coalition as was again demonstrated with the removal of Malcolm Turnbull. Australia cannot continue in this fashion. We'll look at the detail of the four referendum proposals of 1988 below. The question of what could be put to the people in a Referendum as a first serious attempt to "update" the Constitution was clearly problematical. Considerable debate occurred as it was held that the Constitution was still "encased" in British constitutional law and practices. Certainly, a majority of Coalition politicians, at that time, were reluctant to modernise that basic set of rules. The limitations of the amendment section 128 also became obvious. The passing of the (British) Australia Act (s) of 1986, presumably ensuring Australia's complete independence from Britain, gave rise to much discussion among constitutional lawyers but apparently somehow it was still not convincing. The following four questions were finally put to the voters in 1988:

1. Constitution Alteration (Parliamentary Terms) 1988 proposed to alter the Australian constitution such that Senate terms be reduced from six to four years, and House of Representative terms be increased from three years to four years; and that (for the fourth time) Senate and House elections occur simultaneously.

2. Constitution Alteration (Fair Elections) 1988 proposed to enshrine in the constitution a guarantee that all Commonwealth, State and Territory elections would be conducted democratically.

3. Constitution Alteration (Local Government) 1988 proposed to alter the constitution to recognise local government.

4. The Constitution Alteration (Rights and Freedoms) 1988 was proposed legislation that was would improve the human rights protections.

Even though contrary to federal structural theory what an extremely encouraging step it was to try to improve on the Cinderella status of local government in the federation! (In a federation local government is the **second** tier of state governments, not the **third** tier of the federal government).

The fourth question embodied much of the concerns of the committee: the proposal sought to enshrine in the Australian constitution various civil rights, including freedom of religion, rights in relation to trials, and rights regarding the compulsory acquisition of property.

Initially, three of the proposals, put by the Hawke Government, had tentative bi-party support for these proposals, but this was withdrawn altogether during the campaign. In the end, the Coalition parties opposed all four proposals. The highest national vote was 37.6 % for the "Fair Elections" question, a sad result. Once again it was demonstrated that constitutional referenda fail unless they have the full support from both major parties. *After this debacle these major parties basically gave up for the next 32 plus years!* Currently, the Australian Law Reforming Commission is re-visiting the need for constitutional reform as the lead issue of wider Law Reform. The author has submitted a formal proposal to rewrite the Constitution entirely. It really is the only way to resolve the issue. The piecemeal tinkering strategy in relation to the Constitution has failed consistently, often as a result of the combination of federation, section 128 and the two-party system! Only wholesale change here will remove these barriers.

Looking at all four proposals, and that they were knocked back by the conservative Coalition, the question also arises was this really a demonstration of true conservatism? The answer would seem to be hardly! The opposition was reactionary! Would these proposals have been knocked back by a more broadly representative Parliament? Probably not. Which, of course, leads one to question the electoral system that yields such a two-party adversarial Parliament; as Donald Horne once referred to it as *The Winner Take All* system. This could hardly be called proper, sensible conservatism. The proposals were plainly common-sense long overdue reforms, unquestionably benefitting the society. The result meant a halt to piecemeal updating of the Australian Constitution **for more than a generation.** Australia is still solidly caught in this conundrum. It will take unusual measures to get out of it. And also, a pragmatic and comprehensive approach to achieve change.

Earlier there had been a failed proposed amendment which would have improved Section 128 (the amendment section). This was a proposal initiated by the Whitlam government, in 1974, a truly important reform attempt. The failed recommendation would have altered the requirement that if an equal number of states approved and disapproved of a proposed change, but a majority of electors nationally approved, then the referendum would succeed. In other words, the requirement that there has to be a majority of states approving would have changed.

The Constitutional Commission, which had been established by the Hawke Government in 1985, recommended in its final report in 1988 that Section 128 be altered to allow the parliaments of the states to initiate referendums by passing bills containing a proposed change. Under the proposed procedure, if at least half of the states, with combined population amounting to at least half the Australian population, passed bills proposing the same amendment within a 12-month period, then the Governor-General would be obliged to put the proposal to a referendum in the same way as if the federal parliament had made the proposal. However, this was not followed up in the Referendum questions. There were other possible issues considered. E.g. the Commission also recommended against the introduction of an electors' initiative system (as used in Switzerland and several states of the US), "because it viewed such a system as being at odds with the Australian traditions of responsible and representative government and because it regarded such processes as often being dominated by professional campaigners rather than ordinary electors, and because of the risk of tyranny of the a majority". Could one argue that the time has come that the people should question "the Australian traditions of responsible and representative government"? I would think so!

One could hardly regard this Constitutional Commission as a radical body. It is to be hoped that the current Australian Law Reform Commission, as far as the Constitution is concerned, comes up with some really radical reforms, like the option to rewrite the entire Constitution. More about the frozen Constitution later in this book (in Chapter 7).

If Australia is to have another Republic campaign, given the distrust of politicians, the key questions to be resolved would now have to be: *What kind of Republic does Australia really want?* That is a very different proposition altogether, as compared to 1999. A Republic would now probably the last issue to be decided; conceivably it would go through almost naturally, and logically. There is now so much else that requires governance system reform that the lead up to a Republic promises to be something like requiring a public education revolution.

There have been other attempts to strike a deal on what could perhaps be regarded as governance systems. Some regard the Accord of 1983 struck between the Hawke Government and the conservative parties as a relatively successful compact arranged in a National Economic Summit at the beginning of his first term as PM. In a recent *The Monthly* article Richard Cooke wrote that "the Hawke Government, unions and the Opposition built a near-unanimous 'Accord' that still defines Australian economic conditions nearly 40 years later". That may be so, but the deal was one of a conservative nature, a compromise between traditional employers and union interests. Given that the union density has declined significantly since then (it now is 14%) what does that tell us now? Could one say that the ACTU is not representative of 86% of the work force, that they are in fact not represented? While that may not be correct, the situation presents a convincing case for a quite different, a more much direct case for employee representation in the workplace!

The need for workplace democracy presents itself one could say.

In this article *"Descent from the Summit – Looking back on Kevin Rudd's 2020 vision"* Cooke primarily deals with the spectacular week-end meeting of no less than 1000 carefully selected representatives to hammer out a new future for Australia between 2008 and 2020. "Thinking Big" was the slogan of the ambitious conference that was asked to apply itself to 10 themes: *productivity, economy, sustainability and climate change, rural Australia, health and ageing, communities and family, Indigenous Australia, creative Australia, Australian governance, and security and prosperity.*

This apparently progressive venture happened in an atmosphere of optimism, soon after Rudd had a convincing election win, and had apologised to the Indigenous people, but it is now almost forgotten. It did not result in any major governance system reforms. It did result in the National Disability Insurance Scheme and encouraged the ABC to start the ABC Kids channel. "But few of the summit's major ideas were new", according to Cooke, although the Asia-oriented future was perhaps a new direction of thinking. Rudd, of course, proceeded with successfully battling the Global Financial Crisis, by encouraging spending to promote business, rather than contracting, but this was apparently not much discussed at the Summit. It was the logical Keynesian approach, feared by the Coalition, but applied successfully after WWII in many countries. While "progressive' in orientation and style, the Summit produced hundreds of ideas in its final Report in bullet-point fashion, but it did NOT touch much on governance systems. However, remarkably, one such bullet-point was *"Abolition of state governments, with them being replaced by regional provinces".* However, this was not taken up by the Rudd Government or the subsequent Gillard ALP Government.

Mark Drummond, a co-convener of a community group Beyond Federation, analysed some of the outcomes of the Australian 2020 Summit. He found that of 790 people who entered submissions to the Governance stream, about 343 contained content that were at least partly relevant to Beyond Federation objectives, including about 134 that either explicitly called for the abolition of state governments or called for reforms very close to abolition. It should be noted that the project did not specifically have Reforming or Replacing the Federation on the program. Given that omission the response was even more remarkable. Rudd failed to present that issue as one that required discussion at such an important gathering and including action by the Government or internally by the ALP. One could say, considering the conservative attitudes of at least three ALP State Premiers, the late John Bannon, John Brumby and Steve Bracks, that the ALP had given up on abolishing the states, long a key policy by that party. The party has clearly become more conservative but the problems of federalism have not gone away.

During the COVID-19 Pandemic several new questions have arisen that make the replacement of the costly federation highly commendable.

The ALP's recent promise of discussing New Policy – a report.

Following the shock election loss by the ALP, in May 2019, a recent Conference in Sydney organised by the Chifley Research Centre, the ALP's official Think Tank, had a reasonably promising start. Hopefully, there is much more to come. Some 350 members, sympathisers and former members came together for a weekend of in-depth speeches by party leaders, MPs, former MPs, sympathetic sponsors and foreign experts. In addition, there were the informal conversations in-between sessions. This well-prepared and well-managed conference took place in the NSW Teacher Education Auditorium in Sydney on 7 and 8 December. This was not to be a re-run of the 92- page Review of the May 2019 election with that surprising outcome, and it was not, although its recommendations were discussed in one of the sessions by the authors. It was not meant to be, as the official program explained it and President Wayne Swan stated in the opening address, a time for further introspection. Swans stressed "It is a time to look ahead ....it is the spirit of renewal that brings us all together." In the program there were no less than 107 speakers' bios listed, including the panellists. This short report cannot do justice to all their contributions. It concentrates on some aspects and on some remarkable issues hardly or not mentioned at all, conceivably a result of the so-called "echo-chamber effect".

Nevertheless, that desire for renewal of sorts appeared to be frankly demonstrated in the very first session which was a quite detailed analysis of the reality of climate change and the prognosis by the US economic and social theorist Jeremy Rifkin (who addressed the meeting via video link). He discussed the radical changes in attitude by several major US corporations accepting climate change as real and requiring action. He detailed their comprehensive about-face as the driving force of major new revolutionary strategic decisions. Also pointed to the huge profits expected to be made and the large number of new jobs to be created. Rivkin is the author of *"The Third Industrial Revolution"* and *"The Green New Deal"*. Copies of the latter book (2018) were on sale at the Conference.

Chifley Research CEO, Brett Gale, opening this first session, and a well-qualified panel of ALP's environmental specialists, presented further convincing arguments why the ALP needed to embrace this philosophy, lock, stock and barrel. It should become a strong Green party it was argued, or even the "true Green party", the suggestion being that its credentials were already considerable in this respect. Some quite critical views about the Australian Greens were heard, which is understandable in the light of historic clashes between the two parties and Bob Brown's excursion into Queensland prior to the 2019 federal election. However, the ALP's traditional strength and expertise is in political economy, wages, health, industrial relations and human rights. This session at once brought to the fore a need to cooperate with the Greens as has happened in several social democracies in Europe. This certainly would also require the Greens to drop their, at times, "absolutist" (puritan) positions which can be neither helpful to themselves nor to the ALP and, even more important still, **is detrimental to the nation as a whole**. If they cannot accept this their potential for being a partner in Government will diminish rather than grow. Hopefully, the new leader Adam Bandt will address this issue soon by supporting more actively the need for electoral change. No doubt the proportional representation electoral systems in European countries both necessitate and facilitate coalition formation with the Greens, unlike the Single Member District systems here (except Tasmania). It would seem very desirable, possibly essential, to consider a new electoral policy for both the Greens and ALP altogether. This is where system renewal really is required as a first step, the sooner the better. For the Greens being in Government with a revitalised ALP would mean achieving most objectives and keeping the neo-liberal and currently often deeply conservative Coalition out. Introducing the PR – Party List system here, used in 89 countries in the world, would undoubtedly change the adversarial political culture of Australia. **Surprisingly, this was not at all discussed at this Conference, not even mentioned, conceivably an example of "echo-chamber?".** The emergence of an ALP/Green coalition. instead of competition, is a prerequisite for governance progress in Australia. Of course, this is achievable even before the next federal election.

New leader Anthony Albanese delivered a very polished speech in particular calling for the renewal of democracy. Speaking without notes he expressed his concerns about the decline of democracy and the role of Facebook and social media generally in this process. Furthermore, he called on Labor's opponents to respect the views of Australia's scientists in relation to climate change. He also recommended that the dialogue with opponents needed to be civilised and not concentrate on petty point scoring. Listing the priorities of ALP concerns his strong support for "our ABC" in particular drew applause from the floor. However, sadly, the need for electoral system change was not mentioned by him either.

It was an excellent idea to invite the New Zealand Minister for Finance, Grant Robertson to this Conference. The success of the Proportional – Party List system there is very obvious. PM Jacinda Ardern came to power two years ago as the head of a Coalition Government of NZ Labour, Greens and the Indigenous party, New Zealand First. Truly, an example to follow in Australia one would think. The session was aptly named "**The only Light on the Hill**"! One would have thought that this "Light on the Hill" would have suggested questions at least about the electoral system, which made Jacinda Ardern's election as PM possible, but there were none. This demonstrated again that the ALP is a deeply conservative party in the sense that they fail to see a new role for itself as a leader of coalition of progressive parties.

A session on "What would Hawke have done" yielded several suggestions. Hawke's strong support for the abolition of Federation yielded the response that this would be impossible as "the states would block it in a referendum". If so, why? Would it perhaps not require a new flexible Constitution first? With Ministers selected from the entire society rather than the Parliament? The recommendation of workplace democracy in the *Australia Reconstructed Report* (1987), rejected then by Hawke as "not being part of our culture", a conservative step that t proved to be as well.

The contribution by ACTU Secretary Sally McManus was spirited but, regrettably, also very traditional. As the first female Secretary of the ACTU, in itself certainly an important break-through, she has to address the huge decline in union membership in difficult circumstances. Sub-contracting, new ways of working involving avoiding union involvement in neo-liberal practices, and growing numbers of part-time workers in non-traditional industries, have reduced the union reach. Therefore, what could and should be pursued is stimulating workplace democracy and also employee share ownership-ownership, the combination of which has proven to be winning combinations for productivity. Sally did not mention that at all in her address. It is to be hoped that the ACTU team of Sally McManus and her advisor Greg Combet, negotiating with Scott Morrison and Industrial Relations Minister Christian Porter on five aspects of employee/employer cooperation, can move beyond the traditional oppositionism and values of the past.

Modernising the Constitution was mentioned by just one speaker (Rebecca White MP, Tasmania?) but modernising is not enough because it suggests further piecemeal tinkering and organising usually unsuccessful referendums. The Constitution itself has to be **rewritten** and be made much more flexible, a prerequisite for any further adjustments. **Nobody mentioned that either.**

There was a session "What voters want", potentially a useful, even necessary investigation for any political party. Clearly, the major parties failed to a large extent in recent federal elections as they gained only 42% (LP) and 33% ALP of the primary votes in the May election. Add to this that the number of minor parties has risen dramatically in the last three federal elections. There are now around 55 to 65, although many do not participate in elections, or only in some seats. To form a new party is quite a job and run it in a campaign effectively is an even bigger involvement and financial task. The chance of success is very small. What does that mean? Voters are unhappy with the two-party system. They want a system that offers much more diversity in representation, and quality politicians. You may not hear that in the "echo-chamber" of the major parties, but the truth is unmistakable.

Yes, the ALP could be, should be a lot bolder in new policy formulation and go public with it. There is widespread concern about the growing inequality of incomes. One would think that this is especially the ALP's province to tackle. In 2009 the party initiated an inquiry into extremely high executive salaries and bonus packages of corporations. It had some effect but not enough. Outrageous salary packages have been paid to the banks' CEOs and other well-known corporations. (The recent iCare corporation executive debacle in NSW and their renumerations is a further example.) There is NO correlation between achievement and sky-high executive salaries. This has been well researched and was proven again by the Royal Commission into Banks and the recent drama with Westpac. If the ALP wants a make a substantial difference it should adopt as policy that CEOs total packages are related to average wage levels by a multiple of that figure, befitting an egalitarian society!

A final session "The Politics of climate change – a wicked challenge" was well attended, chaired by Jay Weatherill (former SA Premier). This was obviously a more nuanced approach than in the very first session where the ALP was presented as possibly becoming the (only) true Green Party. What is Labor to do in respect of the coal communities of Queensland? Here several speakers realistically, although hesitatingly, opted to consider cooperation with the Greens in spite of former misgivings, as a solution for the good of the country.

The Conference was closed by Tanya Plibersek. I had a short discussion with her before that about the desirability of moving to proportional representation – party list system. Her status in the party and her sensible speech guaranteed a fitting finale to a weekend that could open up new pathways to political recovery for the ALP and Australia.

"Bold New policy" on governance system change clearly is still to come, hopefully; there was not much mention of that at this Conference. Clearly, in their own policy areas, the ALP is a conservative party. It is not as yet moving beyond its set of policy ambitions. In fact, thinking of federation, in practice it has moved away from replacing it. That has to change.

The still strong class orientation of the political system is totally out of date. It belongs to the pre-WWII period, if not to the 19th century. Compared to most modern European countries Australia's ALP, with the exception of the Whitlam period, politically is 50 years behind. Australia, meanwhile, has become a middle-class society with great ethnic differences, something unique in the Western world. This has developed almost outside the class-oriented political realm – and in spite of it. Remarkably, the enormous influx of immigrants, especially non-Anglo migrants, refugees, Asian migrants, Chinese students, etc. has turned this country into a 21st century pioneer, with the major parties trailing far behind.

As a former member of the ALP, and twice candidate for the Federal seat of Richmond (in the late 1980s), I gave up on listening to branch debates about class struggles and, later, culture wars. All this mostly belongs to a different era. This is not to say that the ALP is not playing its part as the party of old to look after the poorly paid, unemployed, women, the sick and the worker, but it has to become much more than that. In the European countries social democratic parties are invariably in Coalition with one or, often, more minor parties, including the Greens. The idea here, still broadly held, that the ALP "has to govern in its own right" is a deeply conservative position that has to go. Sure, that is related to the archaic electoral system, and that has to go as well. Donald Horne, writing in **Beyond the Lucky Country, (1976)** argued that Australia still had to "earn its democracy"; that it has benefitted from circumstances and benefits not of their own making, as a semi-colonial nation. A year later he wrote, with other UNSW Political Science academics, "*Change the Rules*" referring to the archaic Constitution and the sacking of the progressive Whitlam Government by the old colonial elites. The two-party structure has thankfully often been checked by a more diverse Senate. It was elected on the basis of a more democratic electoral system, with sufficient power to stop the worst of the duopoly.

Both Keating and later Howard even wanted to reduce the Senate's power but failed. Nevertheless, the time has come now to match the entire political system with the society as it is, in a democratic fashion.

The period of Whitlam may seem to have been a period of long overdue innovation in 1972. It was, but the political establishment of the period had great difficulty accepting it. In fact, they refused to do just that. The *"It's time"* election slogan suggested a great need for reforms, as seen by the party and the voters. Several Whitlam reforms that were passed into law were indeed encouraging. But both the reforms and perhaps even the speed with which Whitlam introduced them certainly frightened the conservative horses. There were some difficulties with some of his Ministers – e.g. the Khemlani loans affair in 1974/5. These were liabilities. The attitude and ambitions of the then Governor-General Sir John Kerr didn't not help either. The question of Kerr's lengthy consultations with the Queen has long been a mystery which have been revealed recently by Professor Jennifer Hocking research who has probed this question seriously and persistently. A recent High Court decision (of 6 to 1) has opened the way to make this correspondence public and what it reveals about the crisis. What emerged has been interpreted by many journalists, in different ways. Overall, it confirmed the deeply conservative attitudes of the Coalition parties and a similar role played by the then Governor-General, Sir John Kerr. It stopped the innovative role begun by Whitlam and his team.

Significantly, even Whitlam's conservative successor Malcolm Fraser, later a friend, did not reverse any of the reforms passed. Still, further modest reforms proposed by the Inquiry into the Constitution, conducted from 1986 – 1988, were all knocked back by the Liberal/NP Coalition. The four referendums proposals resulting from them all failed. The need for a major overhaul has become very obvious.

Anthony Albanese and his team, in their conscious efforts to avoid the traditional two-party adversarialism, need to realise that policies to renew systems are different from hacking on the other major party's policies. Renewal policies would be of an entirely new category. The conservative Coalition Government is basically devoid of governance system renewal ideas. Therefore, it is an area of exploration that is new in Australia. It would go well beyond traditional oppositionism and the public would soon realise this. Such policies would be progressive but not progressive in the sense of left-wing policy. To succeed the ALP needs to embrace a strategy that goes well beyond their traditional priorities. The scope for governance system reform is huge.

CHAPTER 2

PROPORTIONAL REPRESENTATION – PARTY LIST WOULD HELP AUSTRALIANS TO IMPROVE THEIR DEMOCRACY

The Westminster legacy: Single Member Districts

What it means currently: In many seats the Member does NOT represent the majority – and, if not in government, the minority is often NOT represented by the Opposite party either. It is also plainly wrong to claim that a local MP represents all voters in an electoral district while the adversity of the major parties is on display daily! Overall, the Single Member District (SMD) system inherently results essentially in a two-party adversarial system. Minor parties and Independents usually won't be elected. Independents mostly emerge by breaking away from a major party – only AFTER they have gained recognition as an effective politician. Even the Greens, receiving between 9% and 14%, have only had two MPs in the Federal Parliament: Michael Organ and Adam Bandt, separately. Clearly, the desire for the representation of diversity has grown steadily. Judith Brett found that "Since the 1990s the number of seats decided by preferences has increased markedly. Thirty-one in 1983, sixty-three in 1993, eighty-seven in 2001, in 2016 an astonishing 102 out of 150 seats." However, this political science professor does not think that the electoral system is the cause of many of Australia's political problems. This is not atypical of many political scientists who have grown up with the notion that what we have is a great electoral system. This is a major problem in itself!! Indeed, Brett's otherwise very commendable analysis of problems of an economic and industrial policy nature, specifically excludes the electoral system as a problem area. However, in the May 2019 federal election only 18 seats out of 151 seats were declared on first preferences!

Coalition 41.44%, ALP 33.34%, Greens 10.40%. Neither major party has an overall mandate.

Her own report on first preference percentages in recent previous federal elections provides unmistakable evidence that there is a growing interest in greater diversity of representation. The current system does not provide that. In addition, the political establishment is still divided into Government and Opposition. This is in itself a major problem.

Until the Coronavirus crisis, the adversaries blamed each other constantly for not being able to govern the country. Much energy is spent on criticising each other. The new ALP leader Anthony Albanese initially adopted a different approach in that he dropped the combative style on a number of occasions and advised his front bench to do likewise. This may be seen by some as undesirable compromise, but Albanese has indicated that, while his party disagrees with most of the Coalition's precent draft legislation, there is little point in drawn-out combat. That is at least a small step in the right direction, but Australia needs to move away completely from this adversarial straight jacket.

The adversarial parliamentary culture, inherited from the UK system, does suggest he is at least on the right track. The system itself produces antagonism. Australia should drop much of this Westminster baggage. The Single Member District system is the very cause of the combative culture. But there are more problems than the questionable majority and undemocratic representation.

The requirement that Ministers need to be selected from these elected MPs, and then from the victorious party *only*, therefore a **very** small pool, instead of attracting them from the entire society, is a severe negative. The result is functional amateurism, regularly on display. Furthermore, the claim, often heard, that the Westminster system guarantees the separation of the legislature, political executive and judiciary is quite incorrect. The Government sits in the Parliament and completely dominates the legislature. The often-quoted conservative MP Edmond Burke defended this as a useful "buckle" but both the Americans and virtually all European systems never accepted that view. Australia should do away with these practices altogether. It reduces the power of the legislature significantly. Simply put, we can do much better. Furthermore, at election time "pork barrelling" is the norm, another consequence the SMD electoral system. We have seen plenty of conspicuous examples of this again recently. This is poor economic management. It also involves much misuse of public funds. The dominant electoral system of Australia altogether generates the potential for corruption by donations from the major parties.

For all the lower houses, except Tasmania, the SMD system strongly favours the two-party dominance. In contrast, in the 89 countries that have proportional representation – party list, based on multi-member electorates, this problem does not exist. So, which are the parties here that favour proportional representation? Not the major parties! Could the ABC start educational programs that enlighten the public about democratic electoral systems? Neither parties, nor voters seem to know much about that. Is education about this also not a function of the Australian Electoral Commission? Does this Commission realise that PR – Party List is used in 89 other countries? Is it time to introduce Government studies as a regular subject in high schools? Could the ABC take up programs to enlighten the public?

The adversarial culture suggests there are only two sides of politics that matter: rich and poor, capitalist and socialist. In other words, class politics is the norm, also referred to as "culture wars". Parliamentary debate in Australia always reverts to that – as does "industrial relations". There is no democratic framework for industrial democracy to emerge as is common in most European countries. Australia is claimed to be an egalitarian society. Clearly, this is more an ambition or dream than reality. In reality political life in multicultural Australia is far more diverse than that, increasingly so! But the growing diversities still have to be sub-ordinated to the economic class image. There are other peculiarities. Politicians who are excellent

Opposition leaders are often not suited to be good Prime Ministers. Abbott was a sad example of this. In foreign relations the Opposition leaders usually play a role – often much to the puzzlement of the foreigners; shadow PMs are travelling around globally as formal possible alternatives it seems.

The concept "multi-culturalism" is often bandied about mainly for political purposes of the Anglo-dominated major parties. The representation of multi-cultural Australia in parliaments, governments, the upper echelons of the corporate sector, the judiciary, the public services, the universities, the police, is still grossly inadequate as a recent University of Sydney study has again demonstrated. https://www.humanrights.gov.au/our-work/race-discrimination/publications/leading-change-blueprint-cultural-diversity-and-0.

Often the effective Government is in reality the dominant faction of a major party in Government. Thus, this group may represent no more than about 30% of the electorate. Here too the recent failure of Turnbull as PM is a typical example. It was mostly due to the fact that he represented the minority faction. When an MP resigns or needs to resign on account of ill-health or family circumstances or dual citizenship issues, as in 2017/18, an expensive by-election has to be held. In a PR system, the one who just missed out at the previous election, on the Party list, is the automatic replacement. No by-election required.

A further drawback is the redistribution system associated with the Single Member Districts. This is a fairly regular occurrence as a result of strong population growth and changes in population movements. The importance of this can be great and subject to many suggestions of interested parties. Especially in marginal seats, where even minor changes can result in a seat changing from one major party to another, redistribution can result in a change of government. It can also be subject to manipulation by governments so that they end up with only small majorities in most seats resulting in great imbalances of actual party strength in parliaments. The most shocking example of this was probably in South Africa when the Afrikaner dominated National Party won office in 1948 with one seat. That government then proceeded to move their supporters, often employees in the public services or the newly created public corporations, through the seats to enlarge its parliamentary majority steadily. This resulted in the strengthening of their race policies known as Apartheid over the next thirty to forty years. Not surprisingly, when this drama finally came to an end in 1990, Nelson Mandela and his ANC supporters adopted Proportional Representation – Party List! This system is based on multi-member electoral districts, usually at least five but often more than 10. The issues around redistributions either don't exist at all or are much less contentious.

Branch stacking is another system problem. These are attempts to favour one party faction over another in the Single-Member-District electoral system. In Australia branch stacking with favoured members in order to elect as seat candidate one favoured by a particular faction has long been practised by both major parties. This can take bizarre forms which has very little or nothing to do with the interests of the voters in that district. It is not known in Multi-Member PR systems.

Australia needs to move away from this SMD system completely but neither major party seems interested in pursuing that course. They seem to have a vested interest in maintaining the status quo. This system is still used particularly in some English-speaking countries: Australia, the UK, the US and Canada. If the Brexit disaster is anything to go by the Westminster system in the UK has little to offer that country either.

Surely, the questions Australians should ask themselves at the end of the Coronavirus period: Do we want to return to these systems for much longer? Or at all! Do we want to go back to nasty adversarial debates in Parliaments? To regularly have expensive by-elections? To pork-barrelling to swing elections? To be represented by someone of the other major party? Or an undesirable faction? By someone who is only favoured by one faction of a party? By Governments that in reality only represent a minority of voters? Surely, the answer is a decisive NO! All these possibilities fall far short of democracy. Australia can improve on them and we should start as soon as possible.

Major renewal: Proportional
Representation – Open Party List

In Australia the SMD system was somewhat improved by the introduction of preferencing in 1918, made compulsory in 1924. This overcame the original problem of the First-Past-the-Post aspect of the UK system, still in use there, whereby seats can be won on quite small minority votes. Hence the "Australian vote" seemed attractive as a far superior alternative but it wasn't really. However, it was a minor improvement. A fairly recent referendum, initiated by the LibDems held in the UK to achieve that, failed. Unbelievably, for a member of the European Union then, the "reformers" did not look across the Channel where PR – Party list is common! How is this possible really? Strangely, similar movements are now also happening in the US and Canada, referred to as "rank voting" or "fair voting". However, a REAL improvement has happened in New Zealand when it held a Royal Commission into the voting system, in the mid 1980s, which recommended Proportional Representation – Party List with two votes, one national and one local (known as Mixed Member Proportional), a proportional system similar to what is used in Germany, a major improvement indeed. It was first used in the 1996 election.

Australia uses the Hare-Clark system for the Senate, Tasmania, ACT and the NSW Legislative Council. It is also based on multi-member districts. Hare-Clark was introduced first in Tasmania in 1907 and in the Senate in 1949. That system is used in very few countries (4). It requires extensive preferencing across candidates as well as parties, a serious drawback in large assemblies and modern states. Voters soon had major problems with the extensive preferencing. In 1983 the Senate system was changed in that "above the line" and "under the line" options were offered. Not surprisingly, 90% of voters opted for "above the line". However, the system was conducive to "gaming" by parties – about which the voting public knew little. A half-baked reform was introduced in 2016 which still requires 6 or 12 compulsory preferences to be made, making it possible for some Senators to be elected on very small primary votes. The Hare-Clark system is simply not suited to achieve fair and democratic proportional representation in modern societies operating with large modern parties. In the 2019 NSW

Legislative Council election, also using Hare-Clark, only 2% of the voters voted below the line. Surely, the message should be obvious.

The superior remedy is introducing **Proportional Representation – Open Party List.** Voters **have just one vote** and can choose one (only) candidate from among several parties. Essentially a quota must be achieved by any party candidate, the total number of votes divided by the number of seats. A party that gains say 10 times the quota will be represented by 10 of its candidates. In most cases a party – or Independent – needs to achieve an entry threshold to gain representation: usually 3% – 5% of the total vote. This prevents too large a number of parties participating in the election. In the **Open** Party List System voters can select any candidate on the party's list they prefer. In the **Closed** system voters accept the rank order decided by the particular party they favour – mostly they'll vote for the number one on the list. If after the election an MP resigns, the one next on the list during the election will automatically be elected. There are no by-elections. There is no pork-barrelling either.

The voters are democratically represented. After the election the larger parties will negotiate with smaller parties to form Government. There is no official Opposition, MPs are not positioned in Parliament in the Westminster style – opposite to each other. Furthermore, **the government is generally NOT part of the legislature.** Some Ministers may sit in the legislature when draft legislation is discussed but they have no vote, are not members of the legislature, do not shout at their shadow opposites on the other side of the chamber. **Above all, this is a system that results in Governments representing the broad centre of society.** Also, the culture of this system is achieving effective Coalition Government as well as majority Government. This always requires a search for cooperation; and that can take time sometimes. Whilst the negotiations are happening there is a caretaker Government in office until agreement has been reached. Researching a number of countries, the Brit Brett Hennig in his 2017 book *The End of Politicians* found that the Dutch generally end up with the most proportionally elected parliament of all. Not surprisingly the Dutch-American political scientist Arend Lijphart is also mentioned there as the most convincing advocate of the system.

The Senate's electoral system problems need to be resolved in conjunction with those of the House of Representatives

Before dealing with the consequences of the 2016 electoral act amendments and the Double Dissolution election that followed a number of relevant constitutional conditions need to be explained. Australia was turned into a colonial federation in 1901 which provided the six states with equal representation in the Senate, presented as a "States House". At the time this made sense as it was a condition of the less populous states that they should have equal power with the other two, NSW and Victoria. However, over time the eastern states' populations grew much faster than the others. In 2018 about 60% of the total population of Australia live in NSW and Victoria. Secondly, already by 1910 it was obvious that the major party loyalty of voters and of Senators was much stronger than the state affiliation of the Senators. By that year a two-party system was already in existence, a loyalty that continued to grow. The reason for that was that the House of Representatives had developed on the basis of the traditional Westminster inherited Single Member District electoral system favouring a two-party adversarial class culture. This gradually turned into a larger problem in that it became increasingly difficult to amend the Constitution because referendum proposals required both a national majority as well as "a majority in a majority of the states" – meaning four out of the six (section 128). A further constitutional requirement was that only half the Senators would be up for election every three years. In the normal run of affairs Senators hold office for six years, except after a Double Dissolution. This means that half of the Senators are elected in circumstances which could be quite different from those three years later, including the composition of the House of Representatives and the Government itself. These three aspects are directly related to the lack of possibilities to effect constitutional change. In addition, only politicians can initiate constitutional amendment proposals, obviously a serious additional limitation in itself and even more so in the adversarial two-party environment. The case for constitutional overhaul is powerful indeed!

Furthermore, in 1948 the Australia Labour Party introduced the Hare-Clark system of Proportional Representation for the Senate, just prior to the 1949 federal election. The incoming Liberal Party PM, Robert Menzies claimed that they had done this to frustrate the incoming Coalition Government from governing. This is probably correct but Menzies actually favoured proportional representation. Certainly, after that change the Senate has frequently been an obstacle in the way of major parties' implementing their policy platform and programs, both Liberal and Labor. The Senate powers are undoubtedly significant in that it can block legislation passed by the House of Representatives. Various efforts to dilute or diminish these powers, again by both Liberal as well as Labor Governments, have been unsuccessful.

However, one can add that nevertheless the Senate has often been a more representative legislative chamber than the House of Representatives; this is so because smaller parties and Independents have been able to gain minority representation in that chamber as a result of the proportional Hare-Clark electoral system, e.g. the D. L. P., Australia Party, Australian Democrats, the Greens, Xenophon group, One Nation, and some Independents. Thus, it should also be recognised that the Senate's capacity to block questionable proposals coming from the House of Representatives has, at times, prevented them from becoming law; or, at other times, has improved them. In fact, the role of the Senate has mostly been a positive one blocking legislation that was only supported by a faction of a major party, in other words a minority; thanks to the fact that it was elected by proportional representation! In such cases the Senate functioned as the redeeming, compensating chamber, a most important role in the Australian democracy, although usually heavily criticised by the governing major party.

In 2016 the Turnbull Government, following a rather hastily organised public inquiry, produced an amendment to the Electoral Act which sought to eliminate the "gaming" in Senate elections, but maintained more limited options for preferencing. The change resulted from recommendations from an Inquiry by the Joint Standing Committee on Electoral Matters (JSCEM) into the 2013 federal election. That Committee is entirely dominated by the major party politicians. The purpose was said to be to reduce the high number of candidates being elected to the Senate from small and unknown parties on very low first preference votes. Further details about this change can be found on the Internet, Parliament of Australia: aph.gov.au. No less than 66 political parties were registered in 2016, similar to 2013, not counting the separately registered state branches of the larger parties and some smaller ones as well. If there is one thing that speaks from this enormous interest in participating in parliamentary elections it is that support for the major parties has steadily declined. Unless they, or at least one of the two, is capable of producing a bold set of new policies to renew the governance systems, further decline seems likely.

Clearly, there are major problems with Australia's electoral systems both in the House Representatives and in the Senate. Reforms need to be tackled jointly. Proportional representation – Party List is the superior system for larger societies. It is not something that needs to be invented but reformers do have to look beyond most English-speaking countries, except New Zealand. There is a common criticism of Proportional Representation – Party List, in Australia and the UK, that it results in instability. Critics tend to refer to a few examples, like Belgium, Italy, Spain, sometimes Israel as well. The criticism particularly refers to the time it can take before an electoral coalition is formed after an election. We should remember that this is actually a temporary problem. Of the 89 countries it can be said that more than 80 did not have any serious problems. Italy reverted to using Proportional Representation after five years experimenting with the British first-past-the-post system. The principal advantages are a shift to a different political culture, from adversarial to much more cooperative, no more pork-barrelling, no by-elections, more diverse representation, including for women, improvement of democratic representation and majority government. If you want to know why this has not been promoted in Australia the answer can be found in Chapter 1 about the conservative nature of Australian politics and also the lack of political education.

Therefore, some serious crash courses may be needed. This can best be taken up by the media in the first instance, including, the ABC. The Australian Electoral Commission also could adopt a much more progressive stand on this. They do have the legal independence to launch an educational campaign. And the universities surely could undertake short adult education courses. Surely, this does need to be limited to the WEA in Sydney or similar institutions.

Although 89 countries use PR – Party List a few of these countries have had problems with the system. Apart from the difficulty of forming a workable coalition after the election, some of these countries have frequent elections. Others end up with frequent elections or even with governments that are struggling to lead the country properly.

However, there are a number of important safeguards. The first one is that any registered party needs to a minimum percentage of the total vote to be represented. Failure to achieve the minimum level of the total vote prevents the party concerned from having representation in the parliament. This rule is widely used to restrict too large a number of parties. Remarkably, one country only requires a minimum of votes sufficient for one member and that is the Netherlands (0.67%). It therefore is possible to have parties in that Parliament with just one MP (e.g. the Animal Party), but this is indeed exceptional – and has not presented a major problem there. The total number of parties in recent elections has been 10 – 15, although more have participated. Remember that voters in PR – Party List system generally have only ONE vote.

The system used for counting mostly is the d'Hondt method (a Belgian mathematician). The advantage of this system is that there are no "remainders". It can slightly advantage the larger parties. There are other methods which usually results in a distribution of "remainders" which could advantage larger parties more. "Remainders" are votes left over after parties have been allocated seats on the basis of having achieved X number of the quota – a quota being the total number of votes cast divided by the number of seats in the legislature.

However, there are a few PR – PL systems where voters have two votes, a very small minority of countries (4). Germany and New Zealand are the best examples. The second vote is provided to enable local (or regional) candidates to be elected on the basis of local or regional preferences. These are called Mixed Member Proportional systems. In the case of New Zealand, the hybrid was preferred so that half of the candidates are country-wide preferences and the other half local/regional but also of the preferred party. It is understandable that an English-speaking country that used to have the Single Member District system opted for this hybrid. However, the New Zealand people have expressed their satisfaction with the system in a special referendum for this purpose.

Does the current Australian Constitution create a barrier to Proportional Representation – Party List as some people claim? Hard to believe really. In the first place several Sections clearly state that it is up to the Parliament to develop an electoral system. However, in Section 24 is written that the Parliament will be directly elected by the people. What has happened in fact is that they are indirectly elected because the political parties pre-select the candidates prior to all elections, Independents being the exception. This can and does involve extensive branch-stacking even – another serious weakness of the Single Member District system not known in the proportional election systems.

Furthermore, the existence of political parties was not even mentioned at all in the Constitution of 1901. They are only mentioned in the amendment of 1977 to prevent the skulduggery that ignored an important constitutional convention to get PM Whitlam out of Government. The political parties have never been found unconstitutional organisations that violated Section 24.

Likely results of the May 2019 Federal election if Proportional Representation – Party List had been used

Assumptions:

PR – PL is based on multi-member electoral districts in this hypothetical example, corresponding to the size of the six states and two territories. Therefore, the number of MPs of states and territories is assumed to be the same as is the situation now with the Single Member District electoral system. This does mean that the quotas for used for each state differ somewhat. There are some outcomes that are not full numbers and have to be estimated to favour either Coalition or ALP. Overall these outcomes may cancel each other out but may result in minor errors. Furthermore, in some cases a percentage went to the several minor parties who failed to reach the threshold. These have been divided 50/50 to Liberal and Labor; this could be 60/40, or 40/60 in some cases but in terms of seats this should make little difference for the outcome. What cannot be assumed is what voters would do if they only have one vote as is the practice with PR – PL. Under the current system some people give their primary vote to the major parties because they realise that minor parties have little or no chance to be effective. That is exactly what could well change if PR – PL is introduced. A threshold of 3% is used for this example. This means a party needs to be able to gather 3% of the total vote to be able to be represented in the Parliament. This threshold requirement is common with this system to limit excessive numbers.

Proportional Representation – Party List would change the political culture and system quality of Australia for the better.

NSW – Total votes: 4,537,336. Seats: 47. Quota: 96,539

Party	Percentage	Seats
Labor	34.56	16 + 2
Liberal	32.21	15 + 2
National	10.33	5
UAP	3.38	1
Greens	8.71	4
Ind.	4.62	2
Minors	6.19	0
	100.00	47

Victoria – Total votes: 3,695,032. Seats 38. Quota: 97,238

Party	Percentage	Seats
Labor	36.86	15 + 1
Liberal	34.88	13 + 1
Greens	11.89	5
National	3.70	1
UAP	3.64	1

Minors	5.13	0
	100.00	38

Queensland – Total votes: 2,829,018. Seats 30. Quota: 94,300

Party	Percentage	Seats
LNP	43.70	13 + 1
Labor	26.68	8 + 1
Greens	10.32	3
One Nation	8.86	3
UAP	3.51	1
Min+Ind	6.93	0
	100.00	30

Western Australia – Total votes: 1,401.874 Seats: 26. Quota: 87,617

Party	Percentage	Seats
Liberal	43.79	6 + 2
Labor	29.80	4 + 1
Greens	11.62	2
One Nation	5.31	1
All others	9.47	0
	100.00	16

South Australia – Total votes: 1,072,648. Seats: 10. Quota: 107,265

Party	Percentage	Seats
Liberal	40.57	4 + 1
Labour	35.38	4
Greens	9.61	1
All others	14.44	0
	100.00	10

Tasmania – Total votes: 347,992. Seats: 5. Quota: 69,598

Party	Percentage	Seats
Labor	33.61	2
Liberal	30.63	2
All others	35.76	1 (Independent OR Green likely)
	100.00	5

Territories: ACT (quota 88,658 was only achieved by Labor)

Party	Percentage	Seats
Labor	41.09	3
Liberal	31.32	0
Greens	16.85	0
	100.00	3

Northern Territory (quota of 51,750 not achieved by both Labor and Nats – have kept the existing distribution)

Party	Percentage	Seats
Labor	42.27	1
C. Liberal	37.52	1
Greens	10.21	0
	100.00	2

	NSW	VIC	QLD	WA	SA	TAS	ACT	NT	Total
Labor	18	16	9	5	4	2	3	1	58
Liberal	17	14	–	8	5	2	0	1	47
Nats LNP	5	1	14	–	0	–	–	0	20
Greens	4	5	3	2	1	–	0	–	15
Indep.	2	1	0	0	0	–	–	–	3
UAP	1	1	1	0	0	–	–	–	3
One Nation	0	0	3	1	0	–	–	–	4
Tasmanian						1	–	–	1
	47	38	30	16	10	5	3	2	151

Conclusion

The outcome suggests a narrow 2019 Labor victory, in combination with the Greens, and at least three of the four Independents (58, 15 and 3 = 76 seats). Liberals, Nats, UAP, One Nation and One Independent would add up to 75 seats (47, 20, 3, 4 and 1). A major difference lies in Queensland where the Proportional system would have yielded 12 seats for a Labor and Green combination (9 and 3) instead of 6 six for Labor only. The SMD system favoured the Nats/LNP greatly there in 2019. This conclusion suggests that the introduction of Proportional Representation – Party List would yield a much fairer and also much more diverse system. Also, that the Opinion Polls may not have been that wrong as initially thought. The variation in PR – PL quotas is a matter to be considered further. Ideally quotas should be similar. An overall national threshold of 3% seems reasonable at this point. Clearly, PR – PL benefits the nation as it produces genuine parliamentary majorities, majority democratic representation instead of rule by the dominant faction of a major party, as is common with the SMD electoral system. Australians should be aware of the fact that 89 countries in the world use PR – PL, in a couple of cases presented as MMP. Most countries that gained independence since 1945, a large number, have adopted PR – PL. Others, like European countries like Portugal and Spain, those following the break-up of Yugoslavia and the end of the "Iron Curtain" also adopted PR – PL.

The US journalist Amanda Taub published a major article about PR for Britain in the New York Times. She demonstrated that PR – PL would have provided the UK Labour Party with a victory instead of the Boris Johnson's Conservative Party. https://www.nytimes.com/2019/12/16/world/europe/uk-election-brexit.html

There is one further comment to be made. The use of Proportional Representation would further favour smaller parties as voters realise that the outcomes will be proportional, meaning fair! In SMD systems voters do not favour smaller parties because they do not expect them to do well even though, as in Australia with the preferential options available, they do have an option to give them a high preference if they feel strongly about it. However, they all know that the chances of a smaller party or Independent candidate are very small indeed so many just don't bother.

CHAPTER 3

THE INDUSTRIAL RELATIONS SYSTEM SHOULD EMBRACE WORKPLACE DEMOCRACY IN ALL ITS FORMS

(based on a draft submission to Federal Government Inquiry on Cooperative Workplaces, March 2020, postponed on account of the pandemic.)

It is certainly interesting that the Productivity Commission has planned this Inquiry. It was a suggestion I made to that Committee at a similar Inquiry in 2015 when the Committee circulated advance material to interested people. Very important information was that since Enterprise Bargaining had been introduced, in 1993, the level of strikes had declined steadily. While the present Inquiry is still to be held, as it was postponed due to the Coronavirus crisis, draft submissions may well have to be adjusted to incorporate significant recent initiatives by the Morrison Government.

A. An answer to the following questions put to submitters:

1. To what extent do productivity benefits arise from cooperative workplaces?

2. To what extent do employees benefit from cooperative workplaces?

3. What other benefits are available to businesses, and the wider community by greater encouragement and utilisation of techniques to establish more cooperative workplaces?

1. To what extent do productivity benefits arise from cooperative workplaces?

The short answer is **hugely**. I have been able to see this in practice particularly in Norway and in the Mondragon cooperatives, as well as at the Malta Dry Docks, where I did research in the 1990s. This was also the view of the members of the ACTU and Trade Development Council who travelled to Europe in 1986, studied the situation in five countries and produced the *Australia Reconstructed Report*, 1987. The sensible recommendations that these cooperative work systems should be introduced in Australia were rejected by the Hawke Government. In four of these countries, including Germany, works councils were introduced and worker participation at board level was reported. Hawke's view was that they worked in European countries but "did not suit the Australian industrial relations culture". In Mondragon workers/employees own the cooperatives. Employee ownership and workplace democracy jointly characterise these highly productive cooperatives. Several senior Australian IR specialists have visited Mondragon. Mondragon cooperatives' General Managers are not paid outrageous salaries and bonusses either. Admittedly, the Basque people, a separate ethnic minority in Spain, have strong incentives to be economically as independent as possible, but their productivity has impressed the large number of visitors there.

In another part of the world, namely Brazil, we heard about the remarkable experiences of the Semco factory owned and managed by Ricardo Semler, described in his book *Maverick*. Semler visited Australia twice and was interviewed on ABC TV at some length. A very high level of employee participation in decision-making has resulted in high productivity as well as high level of satisfaction by the employees, similar to the Mondragon cooperatives.

In Australia outstanding research by the UNSW in 2011 has demonstrated the truly massive contribution to productivity by high levels of participation in decision-making by employees. The research study is described as:

Leadership, Culture and Management Practices of High Performing Workplaces in Australia: The High Performing Workplaces Index.

It was completed by the UNSW School of Business and can accessed can be accessed at this URL: http://www.hpw.org.au/uploads/5/9/1/7/59177601/boedker_vidgen_meagher_cogin_mouritsen_and_runnalls_2011_high_performing_workplaces_index_october_6_2011.pdf

The Report starts to discuss the questions around participation by employees from p. 50 onwards. I draw your attention particularly to p. 62 where the highest contributors to productivity (out of 32) are listed as follows:

- Participation in Decision-making;
- Participation in Strategy and Planning
- Skills Utilisation
- Participation in setting targets
- Interactive use of Accounting Information
- Responsiveness to Change

2. To what extent do employees benefit from cooperative workplaces?

Again: **hugely.** Their skills are used, their ideas are listened to, their rewards are valued and better paid. This is where employee share ownership can play a significant role. Let me first list the goals and objectives of Employee Ownership Australia (EOA) which has pursued these objectives for a long time now. Given the limited encouragement by Governments there certainly is room for improvement in the policies of the major parties. When I asked the Productivity Commission, in 2015, why they had never committed to an Inquiry into Cooperative Workplaces they said that they had not been asked by any Government ever. Although they have the legal power to do this themselves apparently they have never found it appropriate or desirable to undertake this. There has been a decline in productivity in Australia since the Coalition Government came to power. There has also been growing inequality in incomes over a longer period. The density of trade union membership in the work force has declined from around 55% to 14% over a similar period. This decline has NOT been balanced by a greater say and financial ownership role by employees in their workplaces. More recently, a much greater percentages of the workforce are employed on a casual basis. Several more insecure systems of casual work have emerged. Could it be that Governments finally understand that major reforms need to happen, many people are now asking?

The pandemic crisis has undoubtedly pushed this issue on the backburner for the time being but, assuming that employment levels will be restored, a new workplace democratic approach may finally

be introduced in Australia as well.

Goals of *Employee Ownership Australia (EOA)*:

1. Provide independent and balanced views on employee ownership policy.
2. Promote employee ownership through the provision of information and connections.

Some of the ways in which EOA strives to achieve these goals include:

1. Being the centre of excellence for companies seeking to implement or support employee share ownership or ESS's.
2. Being the voice on employee share ownership issues in Australia.
3. Encouraging research into the productivity impacts of employee ownership.
4. Encouraging government at all levels to develop taxation and other incentives to promote employee ownership.
5. Providing exceptional services to our members.

EOA's Employee Share Ownership Plan Policy

EOA recommends that public policy should be formulated so as to promote employee share schemes for the following purposes:

1. To better align the interests of employees and employers.

2. To encourage employee engagement and participation.

3. To develop national savings.

4. To facilitate the development of sunrise and start-ups enterprises.

5. To facilitate employee buyouts and succession planning.

In 2012 the EOA invited the UK expert Graham Nuttall to speak about the developments in the UK at the time. A discussion about the Nuttall Report, named **Shared Success**, seemed about the *Right to Request Shared Ownership* by employees (a still modest aim). This is a short reference in the context of the Australian situation considering the aim to achieve Cooperative Workplace outcomes. At that time there were reports about a "significant decline in employee share ownership schemes in Australia".

> "As we look to the challenges in the decades ahead, we know our capacity to do better will be built on a more productive economy," said the Honourable Tony Smith MP, then Shadow Parliamentary Secretary for Tax Reform. "A revolution in employee share ownership has the potential to add a couple of cylinders to our economic engine." Tony later became the Speaker in the House of Representatives. He further argued that "for the enterprise it unlocks the human capital of employees; this can drive improvements and greater success; employees who have shares are more likely to be in tune, and part of, a company's mission and success because they have a stake in the outcome."

While specifically advocating the spread of Employee Share Ownership systems in the UK the Nuttall review found that there are three main barriers holding back the creation of more employee owned businesses in the UK:

> 1. a lack of awareness of employee ownership; 2. a lack of resources, including finance; 3. and perceived or real legal, tax and regulatory complexities.

A similar situation existed in Australia with the emphasis on the third aspect probably. The complexities are not just "perceived". They are real indeed; the aim of one of the five aspects of the Morrison Government Joint Inquiry (with the ACTU) appears to be to overcome these problems.

The meeting also enabled the EOA to point out the relative success of Employee Share Ownership schemes in the US, as well as in a growing number of continental European countries. More recently, a comprehensive study about employee share ownership in the UK, providing evidence from 1000 successful examples, suggest that the advocacy has yielded fruits: The Ownership Effect Inquiry (2018) - http://theownershipeffect.co.uk/the-evidence/. The evidence is indeed very convincing. More recent research on progress in European countries is also available: http://www.efesonline. org/PRESS REVIEW/2020/April.htm; http://www.efesonline.org/Annual%20Economic%20Survey/Presentation.htm

Apart from the debate about the quite complex, and rather unhelpful tax situations in Australia, the debate here has lacked the added support of advocacy of workplace democracy. We need to stress the importance of that aspect. The British heritage of IR conflict – related to the politically adversarial culture here as well, has actually proved to be a barrier in this regard. It is truly amazing that in this policy area the ALP has again shown itself to be a conservative party apparently unable to adopt far more progressive solutions. It is in this area particularly that the European examples could provide scope for "new and bold" new policy. The IR culture in 1987 might not have been suitable but one would think that it is now. All the talk about a "fair wage" does not change the culture towards employee participation in decision-making!

However, several senior academics researching and teaching Industrial Relation in Australia have pointed out for **years** how important major reform of the Industrial Relations system would be for Australia. I just mention Professors Russell Lansbury and Ed Davis of at least a dozen. Professor David Peetz of Griffith University Business School made the valid point that

> "If you do see benefits from share ownership on employee behaviour, it tends to be where those employees have also had some role in decision making".

For the most part this has remained largely of academic interest in Australia with a few notable exceptions, as for instance Fletcher Jones and Staff, Lend

Lease (Dutch initiated), and the Nelson Report *"Shared endeavours"* (2000). In some individual cases the enlightened entrepreneurs' personal philosophies drove the development. Most of the examples overseas, with some exceptions, e.g. John Lewis & co, have introduced systems following appropriate legislation. If the Australian Government, employers' organisations and unions are serious about progressing productivity in the workplace, as distinct from continuing the customary adversarial tug-o-war, **effective** legislation is what is required now in Australia as well.

A combination of Employee Participation in decision-making, preferably including staff representation on corporate boards (as in Germany), PLUS Employee Share Ownership, is the ideal situation. It has proved to be difficult for Australian politicians of both the major parties to grasp this truth. Indeed, this reality is an additional reason why the electoral system also has to be changed to Proportional Representation – Party List so that the adversarial parliamentary heritage of a two-party system, representing, even accentuating a class society, is transformed into a much more representative Parliament. Australia needs a new political culture which means that the Single Member District system, yielding one MP per District, should be replaced by PR – Party List, based on multi-party districts representation. We also need a clearly multicultural Parliament. Our diversity is a strength that needs to be seen to work. Therefore, the notion that there are only "two sides" of politics is both false, deeply conservative and simplistic. The diversity of ideas, interests and backgrounds in Australian society is far more complex than that and it is extremely important that any Government is representative of that broad middle ground rather than the owning and business class, on the one hand, and the employees, on the other hand. This old view has dominates our political organs for far too long. Their narratives are frequently about the past. This needs to end. Australia should move on. Both major parties need to review their approaches.

3. What other benefits are available to businesses, and the wider community by greater encouragement and utilisation of techniques to establish more cooperative workplaces?

In this context we might also consider decisions by corporations to move part of their operations or their entire business to low-labour cost countries in Asia to compete more effectively and/or make higher profits. Do their Australian employees have any say in the export of their jobs in this way? If not, why not? Should they have some say in this transfer as the co-creators of the wealth and goodwill up that point? Should they be compensated in some way or share in the benefits of this globalization? These are the sort of questions that are often asked by employees in other countries.

It is instructive to have a look at the Dutch Works Council Act, latest version 2013. This is not a particularly radical Act in the European context as it essentially provides a wide range of advisory, appeal and approval powers to Enterprise Councils; it does provide something that is lacking in Australia where the notion of management prerogative still seems to dominate the workplace culture: it prescribes compulsory consultation and negotiation, within the workplace, not just for an enterprise agreement, *but on a permanent basis*. Management is expected to work with the employees in the Netherlands. Given their excellent record in managing the economy of a country lacking almost completely in natural resources, e.g. it has been virtually free from recessions since WWII, this example could be valuable for Australia.

Workplace Representation (Quoted from the Dutch Act)

Employee representation at the workplace is essentially through works councils elected by all employees. They should be set up in all workplaces with at least 50 employees and more than three-quarters of workplaces of this size have them. (there are other arrangements for smaller workplaces). Works councils are not directly union bodies, although union members often play a key role.

The main channel for employee representation in the Netherlands is through the works council. In addition, in many organisations collective agreements give trade unions at work specific rights.

Every undertaking in the Netherlands with at least 50 employees is obliged to set up a works council (OR) with a range of information and consultation rights (each independent plant is classified as an undertaking in Dutch law). In addition, undertakings with between 10 and 50 employees are required to set up a personnel delegation (PVT), a body with some of the powers of the works council, if a majority of employees request it, although this is rare (see below). Some industry level collective agreements also provide for works councils at lower numbers of employees – normally 35.

The extent of the works council's powers varies according to the issue involved. In broad terms the works council must be informed and consulted about economic issues but on social issues it must approve any changes.

Works councils were first introduced by law in 1950 and their extent and powers have gradually been extended since then. The bulk of the current legal framework for works councils is set out in the Works Councils Act of 1979, which was extended to smaller companies in 1981 and revised again in 1998. There were also minor revisions in 2004 to take account of the EU's framework directive on information and consultation (2002/14/EC); the most recent legal changes were introduced in 2013.[1]

Works councils do not exist in all the undertakings which should by law have them, although they are normally present. Figures published in 2012 in a study undertaken on behalf of the labour ministry show that 71% of workplaces with more than 50 employees had a works council in 2011. This is lower than the high point of 76% in 2005, but the same percentage as in 2001 and 2002 and slightly above the 70% recorded in 2008. The study found that works councils are more common in larger than smaller workplaces. Almost all (94%) of workplaces with more than 200 employees had a works council but only 61% of those with 50 to 74 employees, 70% for those with 75 to 99 employees and 84% for those with between 100 to 199 employees.

In workplaces with between 10 and 50 employees, 16% had a works council and 12% had a personnel delegation. Where personnel delegations have been established this has normally been done voluntarily by the employer. The study found that only 22% had been set up entirely or partially because of a request of the majority of employees.

Works councils are not directly trade union bodies although most have a majority of trade union members. It is, however, very common to find that some of the works council members are not in a union and in some cases trade unionists are in a minority, or even not present at all.

Trade unionists have a basic right to organise at work but, unlike the situation in other European states, such as France, Spain or Italy, in the Netherlands they have no statutory right to specific facilities. However, in some areas unions have been able to gain additional rights through collective bargaining.

This Dutch Act commenced operations in 1979 and has been amended and expanded several times. The tripartite nature of Dutch politics, with a Government elected on a proportional electoral system, tend to give it a role of arbitrator between employers and employees. That is different from the two-party system in Australia, which reinforces the adversarial mode of industrial relations and positions the major parties often as the representatives of labour and capital. If Australia wants to move away from that dated and increasingly unproductive adversarial political culture major reforms of party and electoral systems need to be contemplated as well.

Further reference: https://www.worker-participation.eu/National-Industrial Relations/Countries/Netherlands/Workplace-Representation

For the most part this has remained largely of academic interest in Australia with a few notable exceptions, as for instance Fletcher Jones and Staff, Lend Lease, and the Nelson Report *"Shared endeavours"* (2000). In individual cases the enlightened entrepreneurs' personal philosophies drove the development. Most of the examples overseas, with some exceptions, e.g. John Lewis & co, have been introduced following appropriate legislation.

If the Australian Government, employers' organisations and unions are serious about progressing productivity in the workplace, as distinct from continuing the customary adversarial tug-o-war, **effective legislation is what is required now.**

Recent reform moves in Australia. More surprises.

In late May, 2020 the PM Scott Morrison unexpectedly declared he would organise a meeting with Sally McManus of the ACTU and representatives of employers organisations "to clear obstacles to a consensus on workplace relations reforms, giving union leaders key positions if the forums to decide a deal by September" (SMH, 27.5.'20).

Mr. Morrison "slammed the current industrial relations system for delivering marginal benefits for unions while discouraging companies from hiring staff". He said: "the room had already been booked for the meeting". Further details were announced about what was described as a "Recovery Plan".

Ms McManus indicated that the ACTU would join the process but would set two conditions on any support for change because of below of the low growth in wages before the coronavirus crisis. "The first is: will any proposal make jobs more secure for working people? That's really important – we don't want to go back to what it was like pre-pandemic. The second measure is making sure that working people get their fair share of the nation's wealth". The ALP welcomed Mr. Morrison's decision to set aside the Ensuring Integrity Bill, which was meant to crack down on rogue unions. On TV Morrison explained that he wanted to steer away from adversarial culture if that was possible, as well as from the complexities. Morrison outlined the process that would be followed comprising of five groups, addressing: Industrial awards; Enterprise agreements; Casual employment; Complaints with the regime; and Enterprise agreements for "Greenfields projects" to encourage new investments. The PM was clearly keen on rapid progress. Still moving away from the adversarial culture, commendable, even essential, seemed an overriding ambition although not detailed in any way. The initiatives by the PM were welcomed by the Australian Industry Group and Ms/ Jennifer Westacott, CEO of the Business Council of Australia.

Interestingly, the former ACTU Secretary Greg Combet is assisting in this process as well. Combet discouraged former PM Howard from introducing a new system named Work Choices, in 2005, which created considerable opposition and probably was a reason why he lost his seat of Bennelong, and the election, in 2007. According to SMH journalist Jacqueline Maley, Combet was a driving force behind the economy-saving Job Keeper program and "is now appointed a commissioner on the National COVID-19 Co-ordination Commission, which is focussed on the economic impact of the pandemic and our economic recovery from it" (SMH, 31/5/20).

Commentary by and in the media on this apparently unexpected attempt to harmonise and energise usually combative sides in industrial relations has varied from disbelief, even considerable cynicism, to surprise and cautious optimism. The entry of Combet should be welcomed by all parties. He has also favoured employee participation schemes in the past as well.

CHAPTER 4

FEDERATION, ITS TIME IS UP.
AUSTRALIANS CAN DO MUCH BETTER

Given the expected very high cost of overcoming the effects of the Corona virus crisis Australia will finally have to consider dealing with the growing cost of maintaining the Federation. It is in this area that enormous savings can be made but that is by no means the only advantage to be gained by the reform suggested in this chapter. The National Cabinet, which will now remain in session, together with some subsidiary Councils, should discuss issues like this. A National Federation Reform Council has already been contemplated, but most reforms that have been suggested in the past for the Federation have come to basically nothing. As a pragmatist it is possible that Mr. Morrison will come to that conclusion as well. Perhaps the name of this new body should be National Reform Council.

The National Cabinet was formed to deal with one specific health issue, with decision-making principally delegated to national medical experts. It was an exceptional, specific task of limited duration, which was far removed from the usual Federal-State interactions. To link this to the traditional party bickering over a very large range of political and administrative issues is not meaningful. If anything has been demonstrated it is that Australia is capable of quick national action in a case of great urgency and importance – indeed somewhat similar to a war situation.

The initial response by the public was the impression that federation has shown to work well during the COVID-19 pandemic and how it was handled via the State Governments. This really cannot be accepted as a justification for the federal system. Moreover, several events have occurred that suggest quite the opposite. The Ruby Princess drama was a classic example how both Border Control failed to insist on quarantine responses, with very serious consequences, and the NSW State Government failed as well. The current Constitution of Australia (1901), in Section 51 (ix) list Quarantine as a Commonwealth Power. In this particular case this power could have been exercised by Federal Department of Health as well as the Border Control Department. There is no evidence of that power having been delegated to the NSW State Department of Health but it must be assumed that this is what happened. A Special Commission of Inquiry was established to find out how 2647 passengers were allowed to disembark and disperse on arrival in Sydney. It reported on 14th August 2020. It was chaired by Commissioner Bret Walker SC, who concluded in his Report that serious mistakes had been made by NSW Health officials. According to Walker an expert panel of the NSW Health Department had decided to assess the ship as of "low risk" before it docked in Sydney on March 19th. He considered this as "inexplicable and unjustifiable." The federal department was apparently not involved in his view. While the lack of adequate testing on board was a major contributing factor the NSW State Health department could have insisted that everyone should have been tested and all positive cases hospitalised and other quarantined. Instead all passengers were allowed to disembark. Of the 1682 passengers from Australia 663 contracted COVID-19. An article on the Report in the SMH (16.08.'20) stated that there had been 28 deaths of which 20 in Australia. The spread of the virus in NSW and, possibly, elsewhere in Australia is regarded as originating from this group in particular.

Was this something that should have been left to the semi-sovereign State of NSW? Or was this a national responsibility? The conclusion of Mr. Walker is questionable. In fact, the National Cabinet, put together to deal with the health crisis had specifically taken charge of the management of COVID-19. There was already knowledge of the virus being on board prior to the docking of the cruise ship in Sydney Harbour. It was left to the normal Federal arrangement, meaning the State Health Department, to sort out how to handle it. It can be argued that this specific issue was for the National Cabinet to decide, either via the Federal Health Department and/or Border Control. But the normal arrangement failed badly.

Another example of counter-productive federalism is where several states keep borders closed and the national interest clearly is not served thereby. The Queensland tourist and hospitality industry in particular is annoyed by their state government wanting to keep the border closed.

Farmers along that NSW/Queensland border are also very unhappy as their workers and repair facilities reside over the border in the other state and are seriously hampered by these arrangements.

However, at this juncture it would seem unlikely that the Coalition Government would want to replace the federation in the near future, but the ALP could take the initiative to float the idea as a longer-term objective. Abolishing the federation was definitely very much their policy in the past. A well-known important older text, by Professor Gordon Greenwood (1946), comes to mind here as well. As far as the Coalition is concerned it is not entirely impossible either, given their earlier great ambition to achieve a balanced budget. In any case surprises cannot be excluded now. A new "normal", meaning cooperation between the major parties, especially on long overdue governance system reform, certainly is to be welcomed.

The case for replacing the increasingly unproductive and costly Federal structure has long been strong. However, in spite of several major inquiries about fixing the federal problems, in piecemeal tinkering fashion (2008, 2011, 2014), conservatism has prevailed. Frankly, the results of these conferences were disappointing. These events were mostly talkfests about achieving minor improvements. Both major parties believe to have vested interests in maintaining the status quo, although of a different kind for each party. But it could well be of much greater advantage to both of them, and especially for the country as a whole, to take on a bold renewal program of governance system reforms. One major federation consequence is that there are far too many politicians in Australia: 754, for 25 million people. Both major parties, in different ways, have been dangerously conservative in respect of improving governance systems.

Understandably public servants' organisations fear the possible disappearance of jobs. Perhaps this has also been the not so obvious underlying major factors standing in the way of progress. However, there are of course fair remedies. The question now is: Who or which party is going to fix the excesses and serious shortcomings of the existing system? How could they still look past them following this crisis and the realisation that there has to be much more cooperation and competence, instead of continuing with the endless blame games which is part of the avoidance of real progress being achieved. If the solution of major health problems is to rely on the medical scientists, what about the other scientists? They are here. They have offered their competent advice. What about political scientists and constitutional experts who have studied alternatives *beyond* the Westminster and US systems? Will they be heard and engaged? Or are they actually avoided?

Nevertheless, real savings can be made in abolishing federation. Here is a great opportunity to eliminate the unnecessary State Governments and turn Australia into one efficient nation. We need a lean democratic two-tier governance structure comprising National and Local Governments with appropriate regional clusters as an in-between mezzanine-type level. Somewhat like the already *existing* Regional Organisations of Councils, existing but not given much publicity and financial strength. In other words: not more states, as some quasi reformers have suggested at times, using Section 124 of the existing archaic Constitution, **but none at all!** The incredible complexity that is part and parcel of federation needs to end. The major cities should be part of that second structure with special city governments taking over the reduced functions of State Governments. Regional and rural Australia then becomes the direct and total responsibility of the National Government, a logical, long overdue and highly desirable reform. We can start on effective decentralisation, build up the 50 or so significant regional cities, instead of squeezing more people into the five larger cities. Especially the farming and other regional communities can see progress. The local government sector would cease to be the Cinderella of the existing structure. Of course, it means a completely new Constitution, desirable for many other reasons as well.

The recent abolishment of COAG is itself a step in the right direction. But there are other aspects that provide solid reasons for further major change. Think about the 99 year lease the Northern Territory Government concluded with the Government of China, in 2015. How could that happen? Especially because it is not even a semi-sovereign state. Morrison was Treasurer at the time, and he reacted strongly to it.

The latest amazing deal is between the state of Victoria and the Chinese Government. This is known as Beijing's controversial Belt and Road initiative. ABC Internet describes the deal as follows:

> "It's technically a non-legally binding agreement for Victoria to be involved in the Belt and Road project; the Silk Road for the 21st century that includes new ports, highways and railways across the globe. It is essentially a commitment by Victoria to work together with Beijing on future projects for the benefit of both parties. Mr Andrews will co-chair a group that will meet half yearly. A big part is for Victorian infrastructure experts to get access to the hundreds of billions of dollars of projects slated for the Belt and Road."

Mr. Andrews has justified the deal by claiming that it is good for the Victorian economy. But this deal has foreign policy implications and the Morrison government has expressed its displeasure about it. Given Australia's initiative resulting in a WHO Inquiry into the origin of the Coronavirus – and the several threatened and real reductions in major Australian exports to China, e.g. iron ore, barley, coal and wine, the problem is obvious. The involvement of the Federal government in this deal was minimal apparently. More points were made in the ABC's report:

> "Foreign policy doesn't usually fall under the jurisdiction of state governments, but essentially it will mean a bigger market to sell wine, beef and lamb, as well as an opportunity for Victorian institutions to teach future Chinese doctors. International education is already the state's biggest export."

We need to return to the possible dismantling of federation, given that the pandemic is more than likely a once only serious threat and "normal" relationships and habits will tend to return to some extent. Although bringing down the total number of politicians from 754 to say, 400 more savings would be achieved by streamlining public services. The eight-fold duplications of many state departments' activities would add up to a lot more than the savings on 300 to 400 MPs, their salary, accommodation and transport expenses. It is probably very difficult to estimate this accurately. In any case the speed of decision-making would probably increase exponentially. Of course, permanent public servants entitlements need to be honoured. They could be redeployed or be put on non-active paid service, if necessary. For the sake of overall gain this must be worth doing. All this is undoubtedly achievable particularly as a result of superior digital technology, as well as transport improvements.

Yes, that would certainly also stimulate growth in Canberra but surely, there is plenty more room there, and at more reasonable cost, than in the much larger State Capitals.

All this matters a lot more now that Australia is spending huge amounts on keeping the economy afloat, probably well over 250 billion dollars. Possibly even more expenditure could follow if the two million casual workers, who have not worked for at least one year in such a capacity, are also included. Similarly, many recent migrants, refugees and students, are dependent on part-time and casual work. The estimates of the period to recoup such expenditure varies from about three to four good years to no less than a generation! Given that scenario, the need for streamlining the existing public services surely must be abundantly clear.

There are still massive other savings which cannot be quantified. These include the making of agreements, often delayed by federal vs state interests and party ideological conflict across states, and between federal and state governments. This can be seen in examples of agreements being reached only after very lengthy discussions or falling apart, like the Murray Darling Irrigation Plan; also, in the lack of national planning in relation to the bush fires, two great examples fresh in the mind of Australians for sure. The almost endless conflicts resulting from the federal structure can be read up on my Facebook page, maintained over a period of at least 10 years:

www.facebook.com.au/beyond.federation. It has also been discussed at length by the authors of the book *Beyond Federation – Options to renew Australia's 1901 Constitution*. Much of this conflict is aggravated by the adversarial two-party system and the combative style of Parliaments run by the major parties.

Replacing federation – and aiming at effective decentralisation

In recent years a number of former politicians have condemned the continuation of federation for very good reasons. **Former PM Bob Hawke did so on several occasions.** However, at the same time, others and some change-resistant scholars have argued that federalism still has something to offer and that the problems are either imagined and/or insignificant. Therefore, they claim, federalism can be 'modernized', 'repaired', 'saved', 'rescued' or 'made to work'. In a 2012 text edited by Kildea, Lynch and Williams, various arguments are put forward to show how 'practical' reforms may be achieved. The title *"Tomorrow's Federation"* suggests that Federation will continue but its major problems may be overcome by more pragmatic piecemeal tinkering. This looks much like capitulation; it suggests that many of the authors believe that major constitutional change is simply not possible. A quite different position is needed. Not only is major change regarded as possible, but it is also essential that it happens. There is a limit to this kind of 'pragmatism', if it is that. The cost of federation is staggering and the lack of effective decentralization in Australia is directly attributable to federation. The states are financially too weak to effectively stimulate decentralization in their jurisdictions and the Federal government does not regard that it as its role.

A spectacular number of federal-state money-wasting and looming crises have emerged in federal Australia. They have rumbled on in major and minor public policy areas in recent decades, health services being the most spectacular, transport difficulties a close second. This situation, thankfully, has prompted considerable research about alternatives and public attitudes, amongst others by specialists at Griffith University. The PhD thesis by the Canberra high school teacher Mark Drummond (2008) provided evidence that federal government had become extremely costly and is broken. Overall the results demonstrate that there is much dissatisfaction amongst the general public with federal-state relations as well. Also, a number of research papers appeared, of the conservative kind, such as the work by Anne Twomey and Glenn Withers (2007), which aims to show that some other federations are doing well and that there is no cause for alarm here. Seven years later we know of course that the Global Financial Crisis started in the US, the first modern example of a federation. It spread from there, and that was not the first international catastrophe to emanate from the USA. A conference a year later, Making Federalism Work (ANSZOG 11/12 September, 2008) was mainly about that, rescuing federation. A subsequent Conference in Tenterfield, in October 2008, organized by the Federation Research Centre of Griffith University and the Institute of Public Administration Australia (IPAA) was considering Cooperative Federalism. It was attended by many senior public servants, politicians and some academics. My own paper there 'Meliorist piecemeal tinkering with federalism: recipe for disaster?' offered the view that Cooperative Federalism was no long-term solution for the problem of deteriorating federal-state relations at all.

A later paper by the late Richard Murray may seem to have been a new departure. It was entitled: ***New Federation with a Cities and Regional Approach.***

Murray was a retired senior economist at Federal Treasury, with experience in the IMF. Much of his paper was devoted to improving fiscal imbalance, as have others done before him, e.g. the economist J. Pincus, explained in ***Six myths of federal-state financial relations***, CEDA, 2007.

The Murray proposal had some merit and is more progressive than the one by Pincus who judged the Australian federation as *"the most successful in modern history"*, a view that could discourage younger people to tackle the constitutional impasse.

However, what is altogether missing in the papers of Murray and Pincus is a discussion about what the essential characteristics of a federation are, why it is formed, and how the circumstances of the society it serves can change significantly over time. This can be so drastic that maintaining a once useful structure becomes a costly burden. A federation always requires a written constitution and a constitutional court overseeing it and, in practice, maintaining the division of sovereignty laid down in that constitution. This has been so difficult in Australia that several well-known commentators have described the constitution as 'frozen'. To get it out of the deep freeze, piecemeal tinkering and meliorism strategies are certain to fail. Yet, it seems extremely difficult to exit this mode of operation. Economists and constitutional lawyers approach federalism from a different perspective than political scientists. Federation is essentially a power bargain that is then written up in a constitution. The power relationships change over time, for all kinds of reasons, but the written constitution can drag behind, as it has in Australia, in many areas.

Murray wanted to do away with the states but rejects a unitary state early in his proposal because he equated it with a centralised state. Many unitary states are in fact highly decentralized, organized on the principle of flexible subsidiarity, meaning decentralization to its lowest *effective* level. The notion that federalism ensures effective decentralization is another, widely held misconception. The **centralization problem in this country exists primarily at the state level**, while growing state financial weakness aggravates that situation.

Still, Murray suggested a 'New Federation' as a 'revamp' of the old one, although it seems quite different in many ways. There would be five major city governments and 19 regional governments, named Regional Councils, and a two-tier structure, national ('new federal') and regional. Here is a statement as to revenue collection.

> *"**Revenue powers** would also be clearly divided between the two tiers of government. The Federal Government would have direct constitutional power for raising personal and business income taxes, customs and excise duties, and resource taxes. The City and Regional Councils would be constitutionally empowered to raise consumption taxes, land taxes and congestion taxes under nationally agreed regimes covering these taxes".*

Regional Parliaments – Regional Governments?

However, there is not much discussion at all about the detail of regional parliaments and regional governments. Are they essentially smaller versions of the existing states? How large, will there be regional civil services; how appointed? It seems that local government would be abolished as well! The City and Regional Councils would take over the work of the huge number of local councils (564). Authority would be "**delegated**" by the federal government although this is NOT a federal way of doing things, so why call it "federation"? However, local democracy would certainly end as a result, rather than be strengthened and improved.

While rejecting a unitary model Murray doesn't mention the need for constitutionally divided sovereignty in a new type of federation. This is quite contradictory.

A stronger COAG type body would make some sense in a New Federation but who really wants a New Federation of no less than five City Governments and 19 mini-states (called Regions here). What to make of this quote?

> **"ROLE OF THE COUNCIL OF AUSTRALIAN GOVERNMENTS**
>
> *A revamped Constitution on a city and regional basis would bring a fresh start to how we address important economic, social and environmental reforms in the national interest. **Admittedly, under this new, federated structure, power would shift further to the Federal Government** (emphasis added). With less balanced power sharing, there would be a need for a fundamental institution in which the two tiers of government could come together to forge a partnership between policy design and legislation (Federal responsibility), and the consequential delivery of programs and services flowing from those policy reforms (city/regional responsibility)."*

The notion that cooperation is fundamental to a well-functioning federal system is laudable, but it requires a completely different party system than Australia's adversarial two-party oligarchy. The combative, aggressive political culture of this country, where opposing parties are in government in different states and at the federal level, has frequently made the existing federation ineffective and/or costly. Revamps of federalism cannot be properly discussed without recognition of this problem. An electoral system change to Proportional Representation would need to achieved first.

Surely, it has become more and more obvious that market forces cannot fix the huge population imbalance between major cities and regional Australia. Government intervention and stimulation is essential to give this a start, but the major parties have basically given up. What the major parties in the metropoles are concerned with, at the state level, is how they overcome the mounting traffic problems, the congestion, the pollution, the time and petrol wasting in getting people to and from work, the psychological problems associated with all this, the high cost of real estate and rents. There are endless plans and inquiries, great future scenarios but even if they catch up a little that very outcome will keep more people in the cities. One particular situation assists regional growth and that is when electoral seats become marginal. Of course, this is not a practical solution to deal with regional and rural under-development. A far superior solution is to change the electoral system altogether, away from the SMD system to proportional representation, based on multi-member-districts. This was further explained in chapter two.

Significantly Murray stated that the COAG reform agenda *"has stalled".* That was to be expected; it was a growing new public service agency on a mission impossible. To the extent that it streamlined state differences it actually succeeded in making the case for the replacement of federation even stronger.

What this means is that any proposals to find a new form of governance for Australia needs to be based on a comprehensive approach. The operations of COAG – now any successor agency – would have to be redirected from the current 'cooperative federalism' ideology, mistakenly re-introduced by the Rudd Government in a previous term. The answer is: 'search beyond federalism.' Richard Murray's approach to a 'fiscal framework' and 'federal financial relations' actually outlines that the dominant financial power of the national government makes a new federation of five cities and 19 regions basically impractical. It is plainly dangerous to resurrect such a new federal structure. Let us start afresh by calling a spade a spade.

Beyond Federalism and COVID-19 – a wealth of options

During July 2020 – when a second wave of the COVID-19 was experienced in the state of Victoria and to a lesser extent in NSW – a number of new ideas and decisions emerged. It was accepted that the pandemic would last longer than expected, possibly much longer, and that the complacency that had emerged could not be allowed. Furthermore, the continued and worsening impact in several other countries, would affect international travel adversely for several more months affecting tourism, trade and foreign students numbers. Further examination of the responses by the Morrison Government, following the proposed partial extensions of the Job Keeper and Job Seeker financial support measures into 2021, resulted in wider debate about Australia's economic and political future. Commentators began to refer to earlier major crisis situations such as the 1929 – 1931 global depression and the First and Second World War. The essence of these catastrophic events is that they represent large scale, world-wide upheavals demanding major reconstructions and the adoption of new recovery systems and attitudes not used or known before. For example, In the US the New Deal broke new ground. It involved socialist type of remedies in a country that has experienced fantastic progress through private enterprise. Similarly, the Marshall Aid plan, post WWII, was the opposite of the attitude of the victorious countries after WWI in respect of Germany's war reparations.

In Australia, the decision by the Curtin Government to centralise Income Tax powers for the duration of the war was such major step. That situation continued after the war in spite of High Court decisions that these should be returned to the six states. Apparently both major parties

regarded this as a practical necessity for the post-war reconstruction period. It was the first serious indication that the federal system was changing away from its federal character.

Statements made by Commonwealth Treasurer Josh Frydenberg, when discussing budgetary decisions that he would be guided by his economic heroes Margaret Thatcher and Ronald Reagan, drew severe criticism from commentators, in particular Ross Gittens in the *Sydney Morning Herald*. Gittens regarded the neo-liberalism ideology, as exemplified by these former leaders, as decidedly most undesirable for Australia in the post-COVED-19 era. The record of neo-liberalist decisions in Australia is hardly commendable, he argued:

> "When you privatised Telstra, Qantas, the Commonwealth Bank, the Commonwealth Serum Laboratories and much else, what's left? Selling off Australia Post? The further you go down that road, the more dubious and distasteful your sell-offs become. The more recent privatisation of Medibank has effectively opened private health insurance provision to profit-seeking companies, adding a further problem to all that sector's other life-threatening ailments. The states' privatisation of the electricity industry has turned five state monopolies into three big money-hungry oligopolists and raised electricity prices far higher than a carbon tax ever would. The admission of for-profit businesses to childcare and aged care has hardly been a roaring success (on the latter, just ask Victorians). Bringing private companies into vocational training has turned technical education into a disaster area that's still to be cleaned up" (SMH, 29.07.20).

The growing inequality of incomes in the neo-liberal world, including Australia, although still claiming to be an egalitarian society, has been obvious in recent decades. When it comes to major reconstructions in Australian society this has to be kept in mind. The need for this is beginning to become more obvious by the day. The impact of COVID-19 has exacerbated this trend. Rather than adding to it the time has come to acknowledge it and rectify this situation. However, this is not at all what is happening. As Gittins observed "the people the Libs have most punished are the unemployed". In contrast, "honourable friends are rewarded with big tax cuts".

The amazing statements by Treasurer Josh Frydenberg that leaders like Margaret Thatcher and Ronald Reagan are his idols surprised many. The current situation differs enormously from the problems of that period they faced. Thatcher in particular was at loggerheads with the unions. If she and Reagan were successful, in Frydenberg's view, that is one thing, but their policies as models are irrelevant. It is altogether questionable that there are any models but if there are, they have nothing to do with traditional employer attitudes towards the management of unions. Therefore, Frydenberg's outlook surely is a concern. This Government has to resolve problems that are unique, and no doubt are further complicated by even greater problems internationally, in terms of trade, travel and tourism.

There are several indications that the Morrison Government is attempting to move powers and decision-making on controversial issues back to the states. This is particularly the case on environmental issues.

The environment Minister Sussan Ley for instance has proposed to "devolve" environmental policy to the states, meaning to decentralise it out of the way. She also ruled out an independent watchdog to ensure that the states comply with the law.

While this book is not primarily concerned with environmental policies one has to be concerned with trends away from sound policy which are directly related to the federal structure of the nation. Professor Paul Martin, Director of the University of New England's Australian Centre for Agriculture and Law, asked the question recently: "Do the states have the backbone to properly oversee environmental management?"

Minister Sussan Ley has revealed plans to "cut green tape" by planning to cede the Commonwealth responsibilities under the Environment Protection (EPBC) Act to the states. The states would be "accredited by the federal government to commit to a new set of national standards about development impacts on threatened species, habitat, biodiversity and World Heritage areas." (Michael Foley, "No integrity with new green regime", SMH 25/26.07.2020). These proposed changes would be introduced in the Federal Parliament during August. The ALP opposes this trend. Its national policy states: "Labor will not support handing approval powers under the Environment Protection and Biodiversity Conservation Act to state and territory governments".

Furthermore, Minister Angus Taylor has made new board member appointments to ARENA. This is a very important body created by former PM Julia Gillard and the Greens to assist the funding of renewable energy projects. These new members favour the funding of gas exploration instead, rather than renewable energy. This can only make some temporary environmental sense if it is achieved by using renewal energy in the winning of it! If fossil fuel is to be used it would be a nonsensical, retrograde move. These appointments are widely condemned.

The questionable quality of this federal government to successfully manage a major reconstruction is beginning to be revealed. This is not to say that the ALP is showing telling signs of developing "new and bold policy". While Anthony Albanese, the Opposition leader, may not have made mistakes, Australians have not heard inspiring alternative policies that stand out as heralding the beginning of a new era. Yet, the need for that is quite obvious. Australia needs a major reconstruction. The task ahead is likely to be huge, requiring ambition, innovation and courage. A significant national debt is already a certainty and although the interest levels are extremely low, competence, insight and energy are needed to turn the ship around. There is no shortage of necessary and desirable reforms. The replacement of federation is no doubt one major one as is the rapid development of effective renewable energies policies, developed and agreed on nationally. Under the Kyoto Agreement, which came in force in 2005, Australia amply met its quota but since then, following further Agreements, in Copenhagen and Paris, which Australia signed and ratified, targets are not met or in dispute. Australia should join the progressive world to effectively reduce carbon emissions. There should be no problem with this whatever. We should be ahead of the pack. As a country with 270 days of sunshine each year Australia needs a Government in Canberra that is solidly environment friendly. This is not a state matter. It is first and foremost a national issue. Canberra cannot and should not rely on state policies.

There has been considerable debate about whether or not Australia can meet its Paris target. The Grattan Institute and the Federal Government's Climate Change Authority think not and that it will need more work towards that. But the point should not be how can we (just) make it. We can and should be doing much better than that! Australians should be leaders in climate change measures. The entire performance in recent years plainly has been shameful.

By the end of July 2020 views had been expressed in the community that federation had served a positive purpose in battling the COVID-19 pandemic. An examination of such views- as shown earlier – soon suggest that this is quite questionable. The second wave that happened in Victoria, primary in private Nursing Homes in Melbourne, actually started with inadequate quarantine arrangements in one hotel. Here again, this was left to private security services who turned out to be inadequately trained for the job they were supposed to do. The Victorian State Government, led by Daniel Andrews, who had performed well in the initial phase of the pandemic, admitted that this was how it started to go wrong. Secondly, decisions by the Queensland State Government to shut the border with NSW at Tweed Heads, resulted in considerable disruption and loss of business. Later the decision by the Queensland Government to refuse entry to Queensland by citizens of "Greater Sydney", following some early indication of a possible second wave of the pandemic there, seemed another overreaction, one necessitated largely by the federal structure. Locking up entire states as in Queensland, NSW and WA seems a manageable policy for a short while but in the long run it'll make the entire country ungovernable. The longer the pandemic lasts the greater the loss to the economy.

Re-occurrences in local areas need to be managed locally, or regionally, by delegation from a central national government that can determine the seriousness of the outbreak and decide on what measures locally or regionally or in a particular city are to be implemented. The federal states are NOT national governments, but the nature of a pandemic is such that mistakes by them can have huge national consequences. The structure of federation, based on shared sovereignty, can in fact be a major danger for the country as a whole. If anything, the pandemic has shown that federation has not been a benefit to the country, but quite to the contrary, a serious potential weakness. Some states may have handled it perfectly but if it goes wrong, even in just one, the entire country may well be in serious danger. The "each state for itself" federal ideology can be a major and fatal policy. Part of the enormous infection and death rates in the United States is undoubtedly partly attributable to its federal structure. Another part is the US electoral system used for Presidents, the very cause why they ended up with Trump instead of Hillary Clinton, who actually gained the majority of votes. This is the "winner takes all" system for state delegates of the Electoral College. Clinton actually had three million more votes that Trump. Time for a reform one would think. Of course, Trump's own irresponsible approach to the pandemic has been another major factor.

As to the major second wave that developed during July 2020 in Victoria the principal problems developed in the nursing homes. It also should be realised that nine out of ten were private nursing homes which, surprisingly, are mostly the responsibility of the federal government. Complaints about the quality of management of such private centres have long been heard, well before the pandemic. In this case the federal government's failures became a very serious issue for the city of Melbourne and the State of Victoria they could well do without.

While some conservatives may desire a revival of the old federalism the reality of the developing situation is that further strengthening of the national government is plainly essential to recovery. The current federal government is currently entirely dominated by the ultra-conservative faction of the Liberal/NP coalition following their removal of former PM Malcolm Turnbull. Rebuilding Australia in a comparable fashion as happened in the immediate post-WWII is what is needed now.

Michelle O'Neil, the President of the ACTU is convinced of the "need to rebuild, as we did after WWII, and we must do that again. We need a plan to get the country back to work" (SMH, 20.07.2020). She supports the idea of a long-term commitment to reconstruction, led by government, with unprecedented levels of support and resources.

The commitments of John Curtin are referred to as an example of the scope of action, massive at the time and already started during that war.

Ms. O'Neil calls for similar leadership from the Morrison Government.

She refers to the role of the trade unions at the time when membership of the unions was very much higher than is the case now. She lists five concrete, pragmatic initiatives designed to create and save hundreds of thousands of jobs, protect and nurture whole industries, invest in future skills and training, and strengthen physical and social infrastructure. She said "our plans are: national commitment to free early child education and care, massive investment in training (including 150.000 free TAFE places), a *Rediscover Australia* initiative to help our travel and hospitality sectors survive, a big rise in infrastructure investment and a comprehensive plan for sustainable manufacturing".

These ideas convey the right spirit, but the times have changed considerably, and the projects and detail for today may have to be quite different. She realises that failure to act along these lines could mean mass unemployment, destruction of industries and a much higher cost to the nation "in the long run". It is unrealistic to expect such a bold re-direction of enterprise from the Morrison Government and his team.

There are no doubt major tasks that could be tackled like social housing. A good example here would be the way the Americans tackled this in the late 1950s. The project was called Levittown, centred on Pennsylvania. This remarkable community-oriented housing construction project, built on old farmland, delivered 40 houses per day, to a total of 38,000. The purchasing cost at the time was US $10,000. All single-family homes, with a sizeable block of land around it, incomparable to the high-rise apartments in Australia; these were built fast in a professional way with large teams (36) concentrating on quite limited sections (27) of each house. Prefabricated homes may well exist in Australia today, but construction speed and large quantities are additional requirements, especially if significant migration numbers are to be maintained. The Dutch have also concentrated on inexpensive, entirely prefabricated houses in recent years, both in the

Netherlands and here. Even the Snowy Mountains project was served by a Dutch housing company headed by Dick Dusseldorp, a Dutch water engineer who stayed on in Australia as a migrant. He established Civil and Civic, later Lendlease, also known for its workplace democracy ethos, sadly not followed in Australia. Pre-fabricated houses are also constructed on the Central Coast of NSW, under cover; to do this on a larger scale is just one step further. Obviously, such schemes need to be accompanied by suitable decentralisation of industries something that the state governments in Australia have generally neglected in the last 30 or 40 years. Instead, the big cities have grown very fast. One has to say that is a strange development in such an enormously large country! Indeed, if Australia is to be much more decentralised than it is the national government's role to tackle that in the future. It certainly was a major interest of the Whitlam Government in the early 1970s but after that it basically disappeared from the Federal Government policy agenda.

Other big projects could be Fast Trains linking major East Coast cities, also including Canberra. This could later be extended to Darwin, South Australia and Western Australia. These could double up with freight trains. Fast trains can be built here. In Queensland fast tilt trains, locally made, run between Brisbane and a number of coastal centres to the North. Antony Albanese has a penchant for fast trains but, thus far, several research projects have tended to question the financial viability as independent projects. But how are their benefits actually measured?

And what about catching some of that huge amount of fresh water of the many large East Coast rivers that run into the Pacific instead of being used for agriculture? The water problems of the Murray Darling Plan are an example of the need for effective *national* planning. The Ord River Scheme is an example of a simple and quite small dam allowing the capture of a huge amount of water for growing crops. Water was for the first time captured to be transported by pipeline from Perth to Kalgoorlie to serve the need on the Goldfields (1901- 1903). This was a very controversial plan (dubbed "scheme of madness") but it served an important purpose and is still in use, 120 years later. Originally 560 km long it runs parallel to the Indian Pacific railway line.

The reluctance to build more dams is understandable (there are around 820 dams in Australia) but the shortage of water in rural areas, especially west of the Great Dividing Range, limits the potential for growing crops greatly. Is it not possible to pump water from these rivers, over or through the mountains to the west? This issue was actually raised in relation to flood waters in North Queensland via the Warrego Rivers (known as the New Bradfield Scheme). A costing was undertaken by the LNP but not made public as yet. It committed $20 m. to the research to be undertaken by the CSIRO. One would imagine that pipelines and pumps would be a large part of the cost of such ventures but if electric power could be generated by solar systems the cost could be only a fraction of enormous benefits that could flow from it. Obviously, this would have to be a national scheme rather than a state scheme. The original Bradfield scheme dates from 1938 and aimed to divert floodwaters from the north down to Lake Eyre. It never got off the ground, opposed by governments on the ground of costs and engineering problems. Bradfield built the famous Sydney Harbour Bridge. Perhaps our capacity to pull off schemes like that has improved considerably. Lake Eyre seems quite far away but there are a number of smaller lakes and reservoirs in Queensland and Northern NSW which could serve the purpose and new reservoirs could be built assisted by small dams where practicable.

And how about electric cars? The ALP had a program, managed by Anthony Albanese a few years ago, to develop "Green Cars". We didn't hear much more about that. What we did hear was that all the car industries collapsed, the one after another: Ford, Toyota and General Motors Holden. Has the time come for a peoples' electric car industry perhaps? Possibly even one or two relatively inexpensive models could be produced in South Australia. Is it conceivable that solar power panels on the roof of cars could assist with powering such cars? The annual races of solar powered cars across Australia surely could be forerunners of more family friendly models. Note that many of these races are won by Dutch designed and driven cars.

And what about the submarines now built in France, at great expense, and delayed all the time. In part it seemed to be difficult as the contractual requirement to source 50% of its production from Australian suppliers could not be met. The reason for that was there was a shortage of local defence equipment suppliers. Why were Spanish tram builders involved in Sydney's new tram system? Possibly for similar reasons. Surely, Australians could have done this. Or was as the Spanish contract really that much cheaper or better or both? Are such major contracts not primarily a concern for the National (federal) Government?

Similarly, the bush fires are now very clearly a huge national concern that requires a great deal more attention and much quicker action involving aircraft availability at the onset. Initially PM Scott Morrison thought it was OK to have a holiday in Hawaii apparently because, for him at least, it was then still a state issue. Look how that changed, very rapidly. All such schemes should be national projects of course. Most states are often struggling financially so they don't take it them on. They are not able to take on projects and new policies that are clearly national in character! Thus, federation stands in the way of major national reconstruction and further economic advancement of Australia.

Judith Brett in a recent *Quarterly Essay* issue has discussed the development of the protected Australian manufacturing industry. It was essentially often over-protected for domestic advantage – at least until the Whitlam 25% cut of tariff and, subsequently, by policies inspired by neo-liberalism. However, these have not saved the car industries. Their collapse resulting in high unemployment in South Australia certainly has raised the question. Is there still scope for a manufacturing industry at all and, if so, what should it look like? Here again, the importance of this is a national issue. There are major changes to be discussed and implemented. In economics we need to build on the country's natural and enduring strengths: 270 days of sunshine, grand gifts of nature to be admired by tourists from a growing number of countries, development of an extensive, quality hospitality industry, the multiculturalist society itself, all industries that derive from and boost these natural and permanent advantages, like outstanding transport systems., new high tech industries. Some rural exports follow from major new advantages to growing crops and produce that are wanted abroad – for this more water needs to be made available as well as superior agricultural practices and methods.

CHAPTER 5

MULTICULTURALISM AND THE NEW AUSTRALIA. CONSEQUENCES FOR GOVERNANCE SYSTEMS.

Introduction

Multiculturalism is a real strength in rebounding from the Coronavirus crisis. There have been massive bushfires, drought, heavy rains and floods, and then the virus invasion. This country has certainly been tested. Combined with the lack of trust in the political system what will the future hold? The emergence of political, religious and ethnic enmities in recent months has also disturbed many. The emergence of border security excesses has raised further concerns. Migration is and remains a major economic positive. There is already deep concern about the fact that the number of migrants coming to Australia this year will be quite low. On the other hand, some in the ALP, like Senator Keneally, have argued that the yearly intake should be reduced somewhat. There is also unhappiness that temporary migrants, casual workers and foreign students are not or only partly covered by the assistance packages provided by the Federal Government. In fact, initially some were told to go home. That was virtually impossible as airlines services had been limited severely. Others did not even have the money to do that.

This chapter aims to draw attention to the need for multicultural unity, equality and equal representation of all citizens and its importance for a speedy economic recovery. "We are one, but we are many", Australians sing on many public occasions, and the ABC – TV promotes that idea regularly. Quite so! There is still work to be done though. Restoring trust in the political system and constitutional renewal. The economy is another issue. What will assist here in any case is that most migrants, as well as refugees, are highly motivated to succeed.

a. Multiculturalism as a political slogan – views of Australian cultural diversity, nationally and internationally.

As part of the White Australia policy, before 1972 all migrants were expected to fully integrate and become 'Australians", to assimilate. This policy was changed dramatically under the Whitlam Government. Since then, Australian governments have adopted more progressive policies to promote multiculturalism.

Governance systems that need reform involve political representation, the electoral system, merit-based career promotions and the Australian Constitution. Without such reforms, "multiculturalism" is in danger of becoming a meaningless, political catchphrase.

Multiculturalism, largely considered a major benefit for the Australian economy, has been presented as a positive model for other countries as well. However, due to the ways in which asylum seekers and refugees are sometimes dealt with, serious questions around the sincerity of the Australian multicultural model have emerged. The murder of 51 followers of Islam in Christchurch a year ago, committed by an Australian Far-right follower, has also left many Australians wondering what 'multicultural Australia' actually represents and how a conservative Government deals with this.

The Director of the Australian Security Intelligence Office (ASIO), Mike Burgess, has recently publicly stated that" the extreme right-wing threat is real and growing". The Australian Labor Party has called for right-wing extremism groups to be placed on the national register, to make it "fit for purpose". They are not there now.

Former Senator Brandis expressed his deepest concerns when *One Nation* Senator Pauline Hanson turned up in a burqa in the Australian Senate. His stance was applauded, seen as a courageous public call for all people including politicians to take political responsibility. He rejected her behaviour candidly and quite publicly in Parliament. This was a positive change considering his earlier claim that people should have the freedom and right to be "bigots". With that statement he opposed the Racial Discrimination Act, 1975 section 18c. Was there any public backlash of this? Senator Brandis is now Australian High Commissioner to the United Kingdom.

Although Australia is an immigration country, internationally developments in Australia are watched with some concern and reserve. Kelly Tranter reported in the e-Journal *Independent Australia* on 14.12.2017:

> "Australians are repeatedly told by our Government that 'We are the envy of the world when it comes to strong border protection policies'. Yet heavily redacted documents relating to our bid for the United Nations Human Rights Council, released under Freedom of Information laws, suggest that in diplomatic circles the view is that our border protection policies create a reputational vulnerability, resulting in a defensive position against the increasing pressure of the world. Consecutive immigration ministers and prime ministers confidently assert that Australia has found the solution to border protection issues and proudly spruik this glorious news to all those parts of the world struggling with similar issues. Few take them seriously."

Far-right ideology in European countries ("populism") is growing, primarily due to very large numbers of non-Europeans entering Europe as refugees, sometimes also called 'migrants'. But these countries are NOT immigration countries. Thus, the current Australian "border protection policies" are, in part, inappropriate for their purposes. Australia's border protection policies are not really designed to address an influx of large numbers of uninvited migrants, essentially asylum seekers and political refugees. However, they now seem to be driven by racial and religious prejudices. In principle, such sentiments should have no place in an immigration country that is an effective multicultural society. Australian politicians signed the 1951

85

International Labour Organisation Convention, with that agreeing to accept political refugees. Most refugees now are indeed political refugees as they were in the post-WWII era; people badly in need of a new home and country. Almost invariably, highly motivated potential citizens.

But by claiming that refugee and asylum seekers are "illegal immigrants", far-right policies supported by a faction of the current Coalition undermine the ideal of a multicultural Australia. They also hinder migrants from succeeding in Australia, although many of them are skilled, have excellent English language skills and would add AUD 9 billion to the Australian economy provided migrants' skills are matched with the jobs they hold (BCEC, 2019).

When the Coronavirus drama has been overcome the economic recovery of Australia will need the maximum input from all its people, including its migrants and so-called "illegal" immigrants.

b. The historical development of a society of migrant cultures since 1972.

In recent research we found that from other than English Speaking Backgrounds remain largely invisible due to systemic discrimination and fragmentation, which reinforces the stigma around migrants' competencies. Political representation of ethnic minorities, although improving, is still inadequate. Particularly groups known as CALD (Culturally and Linguistically Diverse), among them many skilled women, tend to be under-utilised. Highly skilled ethnic immigrants, now frequently of Asian origin, experience considerably difficulty in reaching executive levels in corporations, public services and not-for-profit organisations. Achievements of post WWII migrants from other than English-Speaking backgrounds are sparsely rewarded in annual honours lists.

The policy of Social Inclusion, promoted by the ALP after 2007, was supposed to assist multiculturalism. But further commercialisation of the Special Public Broadcaster SBS reduced its role of achieving cultural diversity through the use of media (Pomeranz & Dempster, April 2015).

Plans to merge the public broadcasters ABC and SBS would have further reduced SBS's contributions, and the closure of the ABC's Australia overseas network greatly reduced interaction with and exposure to Asian and Pacific countries. Attempts by the Abbott government (2013-2016) to remove section 18c of the federal Racial Discrimination Act have been indicative of an increasing trend to accommodate racial prejudice couched under the term of "freedom of expression". This trend certainly cannot continue if Australia is to recover from the major economic setback that the Coronavirus battle has inflicted.

The treatment of political refugees arriving by boats and their management in detention camps in Pacific countries, has raised some serious questions about the multicultural values of Australian society, here and internationally. The Constitution neither reflects the multicultural realities and aspirations nor protects the human rights of citizens and newcomers. The absence of a Statute of Liberty, or a Bill of Rights at the federal and state levels is a further handicap. The ABC-TV's recent *Stateless* program portrayed situations and management attitudes which are less than welcoming to refugees, even hostile.

Celebrations such as Australia Day, the ANZAC commemoration and the Magna Carta event represent primarily the Anglo-Australian culture and views of what the country is all about. The desire of PM Scott Morrison to splash a great amount of dollars on commemorating the "discovery of Australia by Captain James Cook" comes to mind as a recent example. He forgot, or didn't know, that the Dutch had mapped the Australian coastline for about 65% by 1644. Perhaps a problem with the educational system? However, we also do have the Chinese New Year celebrations as well as Ramadan. Thus, Australia has grown into a multicultural microcosm of a multi-facetted multicultural world. This presents an important positive example to the rest of the world, in terms of how multicultural societies can work. But, again, recent federal governments seem to have lost sight of that aspect. In 2012, a national Expert Panel on the Refugee Question recommended competently that the Federal Government consider processing genuine political refugees who were temporarily camping in Indonesia. Once accepted, they could have been flown to Australia, which would have stopped the people-smugglers trade. The Panel recommended also that as a matter of urgency, Australia should accept 20,000 more migrants for humanitarian reasons, to be increased to 27,000. In Recommendation 4, the Panel recommended "that bilateral cooperation on asylum seeker issues with Indonesia be advanced". **But this did not happen. The Abbott Government ignored the advice.** Instead "Processing" on Manus Island and Nauru took years without positive outcomes and sullied Australia's good standing internationally. Policy decisions of the new Home Security Department, headed by the right-wing and populist Minister Peter Dutton, suggested the arrival of a siege mentality found in a police-state. It is dangerous for multicultural Australia if this were to continue.

c. Lack of diversity in key leaderships roles in corporations.

A *Leading for Change* report of 2016 provided a snapshot of the cultural backgrounds of chief executive officers of ASX 200 companies, federal ministers, heads of federal and state government departments, and vice-chancellors of universities. It also examined the cultural backgrounds of senior management at lower executive levels and group executives of ASX 200 companies, elected members of the Commonwealth Parliament, deputy heads of government departments and deputy vice chancellors of universities.

The classifications used in the Leading for Change report (2016) were:

- Indigenous background;
- Anglo-Celtic background;
- European background; and
- non-European background.

Using statistical modelling based on the 2016 Census, 58 % of the Australian population has an Anglo-Celtic background, 18 % a European background, 21 % a non-European background, and 3 % an Aboriginal or Torres Strait Islander (Indigenous) background. Thus, cultural diversity is significantly underrepresented among senior leaders in Australian organisations and institutions. Of the 2490 most senior posts in Australia, 75.9 % has an Anglo-Celtic background, 19 % a European background, 4.7 % a non- European background, and 0.4 % an Indigenous background.

So around 95 % of senior leaders in Australia have an Anglo-Celtic or European background. Cultural diversity is particularly low within the senior leadership of Australian government departments and Australian universities. Of the 372 chief executives and equivalents identified in this study, 76.9 % has an Anglo-Celtic background, 20.1 % a European background, and 2.7 % a non- European background. There is only one chief executive who has an Indigenous background (0.3 per cent).

d. Parliament fails to reflect multicultural Australia

A comprehensive and detailed paper published by the NSW Parliamentary Research Library, sketched the situation in 2006 (more than 60 years after mass immigration started).

> *"The purpose of this paper has been to highlight some of the complex historical, theoretical and structural aspects hindering the capacity of parliaments to reflect the cultural diversity of the Australian community. At present, ethnic and racial minorities remain disproportionately under-represented in legislatures around Australia. The debate surrounding the appropriate level of presence of ethnic and racial minorities in legislative chambers revolves around questions of democracy, equality and recognition. It gives rise to the threshold question of which groups deserve representation, and how are these groups to be defined? There are no simple answers and matters are complicated further by the fact that many people have multiple group identifications and that groups can come into being and then fade away. Essentially it is a question of the balance that needs to be struck between the representation of minorities, and the maintenance and development of an overarching sense of national identity and purpose."* (Anthony, K., 2006).

The paper showed convincingly that ethnic and racial minorities remained politically underrepresented in Australia. Has the situation changed much since 2006?

When checking the NSW and federal MPs by surname, in late June 2015, the following percentages showed up:

NSW Legislative Assembly: Anglo-Celtic names: 80%, Others: 20%

NSW Legislative Council: Anglo-Celtic names: 74%, Others: 26%

House of Representatives: Anglo-Celtic names: 86.7%, Others: 13.3%

Senate: Anglo-Celtic names: 80.1%, Others: 19.9%

The SMH journalist Eryk Bagshaw wrote "if Parliament was a suburb, it would be amongst the least diverse in the country" (SMH, 7/12/2017). He found that the forced citizenship declaration of MPs not only revealed those with, often remote and/or unknown, dual allegiances but has also allowed us to see for the first time if the Australian Parliament reflects a multicultural Australia. His conclusion: "In short: no, it does not."

George Megalogenis has recently made several excellent observations in recent articles in the *Good Week-end* and *The Monthly,* in which he portrays the rapidly changing character of Australian society.

In *"Australasia Rising"* he writes, for instance:

> "Chinese in Sydney; Indians in Melbourne; Filipinos in Darwin. Our 21st immigrant waves have been starkly different to any of their predecessors, changing the country's make-up more radically than at any time since the 1850s gold rush".

The diversity is growing indeed. It is the word most used as a term that describes multicultural Australia.

> "For the first time since the 1890s, new Australians and their children – can count themselves in the majority. Today, halve our population of 25 million was either born overseas or has at least one parent who was. The total passed 50 per cent during 2018, based on official data from the Australian Bureau of Statistics."

In "The Middle of Nowhere" Megalogenis suggests that, internationally, our political leaders have lost their bearings in a changed world. This aspect has taken on further significance in the aftermath of the COVID19 crisis:

> "Our ethnic face has taken a decisive turn from Anglo-European to Eurasian, while the multiple disputes between Washington and Beijing threaten our place in the world .... we keep returning to the short cuts of old Australia, with government that errs on the side of parochialism, and she'll be right diplomacy that assumes the knee jerk of American and Chinese anxieties will never compromise our security and economic interests in the region".

Somewhat unusual is this author's characterisation of the new wave from Asian migrants as the arrival of "a new middle class" as happened, so he writes, during the gold rush immigrants in the 19th century. The more traditional view of a middle class is rather different from this new large influx of migrants and refugees. It is related to income levels, attitudes and lifestyles of classes in a relatively settled and stable society. As such one could argue that, despite growing inequality of incomes in Australian society, especially since the onset of neo-liberalism from the late 1980s, Australia's society has become more "middle class" in the last 30 years. Its traditional working-class image has declined which is, in part, reflected in the strong decline of trade union membership.

e. The special case of Indigenous people.

Constitutional recognition of Indigenous Australians has again been given the cold shoulder, following the Uluru conference proposals for a Treaty and an advisory role to Parliament. In a subsequent ABC Q & A program (December 2017), PM Malcolm Turnbull could not offer the audience a satisfactory explanation other than claiming it to be constitutionally "impossible". Apart from constitutional acknowledgement, as sought by the organisers of the Uluru Statement from the Heart, full recognition of the First Peoples importance to Australia is long overdue. Ideally, it should include the Indigenous people's participation in leadership roles and their representation as full partners in negotiations for a new Constitution. The overhaul of Australia's archaic 1901 Constitution, is desirable for this and many other reasons. The Mabo judgement by the High Court, rejecting the doctrine of Terra Nullius, was the first step but it is high time for the logical follow-up.

Turnbull's response was disappointing. It also seemed to be lacking in political nouse. The then PM had a great opportunity to begin to rectify the very inadequate constitutional treatment of the Indigenous people, thereby opening up further debate on reform of the archaic Anglo-colonial Constitution of 1901. The Uluru process, being the dialogues held with more than a thousand Indigenous people across the nation, and the Uluru Convention, were historic in both scope and resulting unity.

It was described by Sean Gordon (ABC 27.10.2017) as follows:

> "It was an extraordinary display of both pragmatism and principle by arguably the most representative and largest group of Indigenous people assembled in modern times. And it ended with a unanimous position — that the key form of recognition should be a constitutionally entrenched Indigenous voice to Parliament."

In a Media release by Government the following explanation was offered for not taking this further:

> "The Government does not believe such a radical change to our constitution's representative institutions has any realistic prospect of being supported by a majority of Australians in a majority of states"

Megan Davis, a Professor of Constitutional Law at the UNSW, and a leading campaigner of the Uluru movement, has published some heartfelt comments on the subjects two years later. The gist of these comments (*The Monthly*, October 2019) draws attention to the huge gap between the Turnbull Government and the Australian society on the subject of Indigenous recognition. We should remember that Turnbull was the leader of the minority faction in that Government.

Bill Shorten, then ALP Opposition leader, offered qualified support:

"We owe the [Uluru delegates] an open mind on the big questions. On the form recognition takes, on treaties, on changes required in the constitution .... and on the best way to fulfil the legitimate and long-held aspiration of Aboriginal people for a meaningful, equal place in our democratic system."

Professor Davis, (also a pro-VC Indigenous Affairs, UNSW) listed a huge array of supporters in the society.

"Many Australians have taken up the offer to walk with us in a movement of the Australian people for a better future: Civil society groups, professional societies, local community groups, not-for-profits, corporations, universities, schools and unions but, as expected, not all of our political representatives".

Well-known ABC presenter Laura Tingle, quoted in the article, also points out the gap between the politicians and the people.

"this group is actually trying .... once again to find a proposal that will work for politics and for the country .... like the same-sex marriage push, had come from outside politics, and was supported from outside politics before it was supported inside politics".

Julie Power wrote in the SMH 29.5.2019:

'Gift to the nation': 14 organisations support referendum and reconciliation.

The Uluru Statement from the Heart was a "gift to the nation" to build a bridge "between an ancient past and a hopeful future", said Catherine Hunter, a partner with KPMG.

"KPMG is one of 14 organisations who have accepted the Uluru statement's invitation to walk the path to reconciliation with First Nations' peoples. On Wednesday, a coalition of companies, organisations and universities will throw their support behind the Uluru Statement and its call for a referendum to enable constitutional reform."

The conventional parliamentary system and its ancillary mechanisms have failed the Indigenous community quite clearly, again. The need for constitutional change is abundantly clear and the lack of guts by the Government can only be described as lack of awareness of the urgent need for change. Turnbull regrettably failed to stand up to his right-wing faction. The ALP's cautious support should have been stronger. They could also have used the occasion to plug for major constitutional change. Neither of these major parties appear to understand this. Turnbull's response could have been to enlist the ALP's full support on this issue. He could have carried it easily in Parliament, in a free vote, and put his right-wing faction to shame at the same time. In the process he would have taught them a lesson! Instead, he argued "it would be very difficult constitutionally" instead of "we will get this through Parliament and, if necessary, will put this to a referendum which, as in 1967, would have been carried easily".

In his recent book The Bigger Picture (2020) Turnbull defends his position in considerable detail e.g. by claiming that an advisory Indigenous Voice outside Parliament would be "impractical".

> "What would be practical expression of the Voice look like? What would the voice look like here for the Yoingu people? What would it look like for the people of Western Sydney, who are the largest population of Aboriginal people in Australia? Is our highest aspiration to have Indigenous people outside the parliament, providing advice to the parliament? Or is it to have as many Indigenous voices, elected, within our parliament? What impact would the Voice have on issues like child protection and justice, when the legislation and responsibility largely rests with the state and territory government?" (p. 572)

One would have thought then that the Coalition might have provided reforms to the electoral system to the advantage of the Indigenous people of Australia as a superior way to have the *Voice of the First Nation* heard in that place. This is constitutionally possible even now. The ultimate solution of course is a new Constitution to be assembled, together with the Indigenous people. They were not at all involved in the making of the 1901 Constitution we should remember. That would also take care of

Sections 25 and 51 xxvi dealing with people of "any race", still in the current Constitution.

It was clearly an opportunity missed! He was apparently more concerned with not upsetting the majority right wing-faction of his own party than enlisting the support of the ALP, thereby representing the middle ground of Australia on this issue. Again, the adversarial party system was blocking sound solutions! The ALP supported The Uluru Statement. Turnbull was informed of that at the annual Garma Festival held at Gulkula in Arnhem land (August 2017). That meant he could have won the issue at a Free Vote in Parliament. It seems so obvious.

The two-party system was in the way. Again, we need a different electoral system! In his book Turnbull explains that he was not pressured by the Murdoch empire and their servile band of senior conservative politicians. He was "his own man" and that may well be so

but why did he not enlist the ALP to get this through Parliament? Could it be that Turnbull felt could not act without the support of his party room? Was this the real reason?

Results of an Omni poll by the Guardian, 30.10.2017:

Sixty per cent of Australians support a proposed model of Indigenous recognition the federal government has **dismissed as having no realistic chance of getting past a referendum,** according to polling released on Monday.

> "The online survey, conducted by OmniPoll in August for researchers at Griffith University and the University of New South Wales, found that 60.7% of respondents broadly supported a proposal."

Popular support for the Uluru objective has been strong all along. Below is a reference of 12.7.19 from the Guardian poll:

> "A strong majority of a sample of 1,097 respondents (70%) supports constitutional recognition, with 33% of that cohort of the view that achieving the change is a priority while 37% support the change but don't

nominate it as a high priority. A further 18% say they don't support that change and 12% say they aren't sure.

There was majority support for recognition across partisan lines, with 52% of Coalition voters in favour, 68% of Labor voters, 75% of Green voters, and 50% of the voters indicating they vote for someone other than the major parties. Support and opposition to recognition has remained relatively constant in Essential's research since 2014."

f. The LGBTIQ community – a popular vote without the politicians

The story of the successful plebiscite is a victory for the LGBTIQ community, Senator Wong and Senator Dean Smith. However, it was neither a victory for the Parliament nor the electoral system. The Parliament had blocked a favourable outcome for a long time. The idea of a plebiscite came from Tony Abbott when he was PM, in 2013. It took a while before Malcolm Turnbull proceeded with it. The same-sex marriage result by postal vote plebiscite was known by 15th November 2017: 61.6% of people voted "yes" and 38.4% voted "no" to achieve marriage equality. It meant that the Parliament would vote on the Marriage Amendment (Definition and Religious Freedoms) Bill and would accept the verdict by the people. Liberal Party Senator Dean Smith introduced his Marriage amendment Bill the same day amidst applause from sympathetic fellow Senators.

The right-wing faction of the Coalition had opposed the amendment to the Act but had agreed to a postal vote, proposed by Turnbull. The LGBQIT community itself had opposed the voluntary plebiscite by a large majority as it feared that it might not be carried. In addition, a NO vote might have hurt a lot people.

The speech by Tim Watts M. P. on 5.12.17, in favour of the amendment, ells a story of the blockage in the Parliament and the endorsement by the Australian people in the plebiscite by postal survey. Here is part of that speech:

"I want to begin my remarks tonight by saying to all LGBTI Australians that I'm sorry. I'm sorry that the Marriage Amendment (Definition and Religious Freedoms) Bill 2017 took so long. Every day that a person is forced to live in our society with lesser rights than their neighbour is an injustice. We perpetuated and perpetrated an injustice on LGBTIQ Australians for far, far too long.

It is right that the parliament will this week vote to extend equality before the law to LGBTIQ couples and their families. It is right that elected members of this place will vote to afford the most basic of dignities to LGBTIQ Australians: the recognition that their relationships are just as loving, that their relationships are just as meaningful and that their relationships are just as committed as anyone else's.

I'm sorry, too, for what this parliament put LGBTIQ Australians through to get to this vote. I take responsibility for the inaction of previous Labor governments on this issue during our time in office, recognising the efforts of the member for Whitlam in introducing the 2012 marriage equality private member's bill and the 42 members of parliament, including the Leader of the Opposition, who voted for it. I recognise also the extraordinary work of people like Senator Penny Wong, who worked assiduously within party forums for many years to change Labor Party policy on this issue so that when marriage equality passes in this parliament this week it will do so with more votes from the Labor Party than any other party—but recognising our responsibility for failing to get it done in the past.

I'm sorry that LGBTIQ Australians were forced by this parliament to submit themselves, to submit their rights as equal members of our society, to a national public debate and opinion poll before we could get them to this point in this place. For these reasons, while I'm glad to be able to vote for this bill, I cannot take joy from it. Historians will note the public celebrations following the announcement of the results of this survey, celebrations that the Prime Minister had the good sense to realise that he would not be welcome at."

The story of the long campaign, before and after the postal survey, is told by Sally Rugg in her excellent book *How powerful we are – Behind the scenes with one of Australia's leading activists,* Hachette Australia 2019.

Ms Rugg (then) worked for the activist organisation GetUp, in charge of this particular campaign, which ended entirely successfully. Apart from a breathtaking count of a period extending over five years, it is an interesting "how to" instruction book for would-be campaigners in other fields. What is also of importance are the political insights she gained from being frequently in touch with Canberra politicians and therefore understanding the motivations of various key players in this field.

So, in Chapter 2 she starts with a definition of "activism" which she describes as follows: *"Activism is about changing things that those in in power don't want changed. It doesn't have to be adversarial, but it does need to make power bend and relent."* Point taken!

In Chapter 3 *"The Bastard Plebiscite"* the story comes to life as the chapter proceeds to explain why a plebiscite was agreed to by the defenders of the status quo. It was Tony Abbott who dreamed up the idea of a plebiscite. Rugg claims that they had driven his Government to a crisis point and that they had no choice but to hold a free vote in Parliament to pass marriage equality legislation. "What we hadn't expected" she wrote, "was that Tony would play us all in a way that wouldn't actually deliver marriage equality".

> "I want to be really clear here: the plebiscite was not a way to marriage equality. It was a delay tactic. Its sole function was to protect and prolong the stability of the Coalition Government who were divided on the reform, by delaying the parliamentary free vote the government should have held that day by another six to twelve months. It was kicking the change to the law down the road a bit and, in doing so, kicking the LGBTIQ community in the throat."

During September 2016 the next Prime Minister, Malcolm Turnbull said "the plebiscite was an election commitment and the Government planned to take all its election commitments through the lower house. But without a Senate majority the Government would need support from Labor, the Greens or nine crossbench senators."

Qantas CEO Alan Joyce pointed out that the proposed marriage equality plebiscite message means that "our Parliament cannot do its job". He pointed out that "our elected representatives are supposed to make important decisions but we're on the brink of handballing the next big social change to an expensive and harmful plebiscite" (15.9.16).

Nevertheless, much to the regret of the GetUp campaigners and many others, the issue was decided by the postal ballot plebiscite. A number of surveys were done indicating that the voters rejected the idea of a plebiscite but, if held, the majority would support the marriage equality.

The Coalition seemed to take this route, at an expense of approx. $15 million, in the belief that the vote would be lost, according to Rugg.

The decision resulted initially in great disappointment followed by an extraordinary energetic campaign and a successful outcome. This is what the bulk of her important book is about.

g.   Conclusion

The potential strength of Australia's multicultural society lies in the recognition of the skills and capacities of migrants and how these skills and capacities are utilised. Given the huge cost of the post-Coronavirus recovery it is of utmost important that multicultural skills are given full reign in the economy and that, to add AUD 9 billion to the Australian economy, migrants' skills are matched with the jobs they hold (BCEC 2019).

But full reign also needs to be given in the political system, even more so. A change to the Single Member District (SMD) electoral system, which has tended to favour male Anglo-Australian candidates in winnable seats, would be highly desirable. Currently, ethnic minority candidates are rarely elected, unless they represent a very strong ethnic minority group in an electoral district. Proportional representation (PR), especially the Party List system, would end the SMD system problems and present opportunities for individuals of different ethnic, cultural and religious backgrounds, also for women and Indigenous candidates. This system would serve multiculturalism. The political culture could change completely as a result. A MAJOR advantage.

The PR system can be simply introduced by changing the Commonwealth Act of 1918. No constitutional amendment is required. Constitutionally, electoral system matters are **left to the Parliament**. This was the sensible agreement of the Constitution makers in the late 1890s and is reflected in several clauses of the existing Constitution.

CHAPTER 6

CONSEQUENCES OF GOVERNANCE SYSTEM FAILURE

There are a number of primarily national governance weaknesses and failures, most of which the general public is well aware, that should be detailed here. Remarkably, some have come to prominence quite recently having been sleepers for several years thereby creating the image that Australia is travelling well. This view is partly based on the fact that Australia handled the Global Financial Crisis well and has had 30 years without an economic recession until now. That situation did come to an end in June 2020 of course, even though it was essentially the result of the economic impact of the Coronavirus pandemic. The failures due to federalism, such as the continuing failure to effectively decentralise Australia, have been discussed earlier.

Three instances of failures will be briefly highlighted here as direct or indirect consequences of system shortcomings. These are not the only ones though. One could make a case for questioning other issues as a consequence of system weaknesses: e.g. the Alliance with the US in the context of the rise of China; the growing inequality of wealth and incomes; and the failure of becoming a Republic, dealt with separately in Chapter 9.

a. The inability of successive Governments to settle the Indigenous issues and rapidly improve the living conditions for the First Nation.

b. The commercialisation of the Australian university system which has resulted in a crisis following the expected loss of foreign students.

c. The failure to effectively deal with the responsibility of climate change as a major threat to Australia's future.

Also not mentioned here will be governance of the states, partly dealt with in the chapter about federalism. Although instances of several widely criticised expensive NSW Government investments, demolition and reconstruction decisions in recent years are of growing concern. Undoubtedly, there are many instances where projects are unnecessary, extremely costly, have taken much longer than projected – failures or badly executed. This is not to say that there not been successes as well. The questioning of competence of State Ministers is the one that is frequently heard. However, while this can be linked to the electoral system and Westminster practices as much as to the federal structure these issues will not further explored here.

a. The inability of successive Governments to settle the Indigenous issues and rapidly improve the living conditions for the First Nation.

The recent sudden protests by the Indigenous people in Australia, following similar protests in the US, have shaken the nation. The massive *Black Lives Matter* movement in the US quickly became an international affair. The initial issue in Australia concerned the treatment of Indigenous prisoners and the much larger percentage of prisoners of the First Nation citizens, as compared to non-Indigenous citizens. The figures put Australians to shame: 432 Indigenous people have died in prison since the Royal Commission of 1991 without any warden or police having been found responsible for that. Several cases of shocking maltreatment in detention have been published such as the death of David Dungai, aged 26 in 2015 in Long Bay Goal. The experiences of Adam Goodes, not a prisoner, but instead an outstanding former professional Australian rules footballer who played for the Sydney Swans in the Australian Football League, were equally telling. The crowd insulted him. The display of racism in the most popular sport arena was obvious and telling.

Many Official Inquiries have yielded recommendations but, in the main, these have not been followed up by governments and other authorities.

As Amy Mcquire, a Darumbal/South Sea Islander journalist wrote in the *Saturday Paper* (June 6 – 12, 2020)

> "There cannot be 432 victims and no perpetrators .... In the wake of George Floyd's killing in the US Australia can no longer ignore our brutal legacy of police violence against Aboriginal and Torres Strait Islander people"

The progress towards recognition of equality of Indigenous Australians has been very slow. Many Australians are aware of it but too many others are not. If they were not until recently, they will be now, and most Australians realise that action to correct this is essential. It is therefore most disappointing and surprising that PM Morrison response to the protests was that he would not be prepared to hold a referendum on the Uluru Statement of the Heart until after the next general election in 2022. He argued that these were important matters of history but right now the need to create jobs and overcome the pandemic were more important. Former PM Abbott, who has had a serious interest in Indigenous affairs, made the point that the courts were not at fault. The problem of incarceration was that Indigenous people broke the law far more often than others, so he argued.

Several other community bodies went public with pleas to combat the new spike in racism such as the Federation of Ethnic Communities Councils of Australia (FECCA), the Australian Council of Social Service, Amnesty International and Reconciliation and the ACTU. They all called for a new strategy to combat racism and placed adverts to that end.

However, the situation is at least in part a consequence of inadequate representation of the First Nation in the highest decision-making bodies in the country. The 3% Indigenous citizens of the total population, spread widely throughout Australia, is a small minority which cannot achieve representation in the Single Member Districts system, as Independents or a minor party. There have been and there are now a few Indigenous representatives in the Parliament as members of major parties, but their voices and interests have to compete with many other issues a major party would tend to give priority to in the context of winning the support of the electorate to win elections. As Marcia Langton once remarked at a recent Garma Festival the Indigenous minority is, in percentage terms, actually reducing due to mass immigration.

The *Black Lives Matter* campaign may well have done more than these major party representatives can do for their cause currently. Although a PR – Party List system, would certainly offer greater opportunity for specific minority representation, this could yield around four representatives in a Federal Parliament of 151. In a larger national Parliament, assuming federation is replaced, that number could double but attention should be given in any case to allocating reserved seats for such an important minority that has been under-represented for far too long. This could be introduced at the very least for a fixed number of years, say 10 years, and be reviewed then.

As far as the behaviour of police and staff of detention centres is concerned the pragmatic answer surely is to properly train police and staff to deal with Indigenous law breakers in a humane way; secondly, all such legislation has to be reviewed as to its usefulness and effects.

The excuse, as provided by one such policeman for his racist behaviour, that he had had "a bad day" when flooring and arresting an unarmed Indigenous youngster during the protests, was an example of a pathetic attitude. It may well be often unnecessary and counterproductive to incarcerate Indigenous people altogether. That would seem to be the overwhelming impression that the public is left with after this episode of angry protests.

The PM has announced that the public "will be given a say on an Indigenous 'voice' within months as the Government intends to create a new mechanism for community input in the wake of the Black Lives

Matter protests" (SMH, 10.6.20). That is one step in the right direction. The above suggestions and this text could serve a purpose in that context.

b. The commercialisation of the Australian university system which has resulted in a crisis following the expected loss of foreign students.

The commercialisation of Australian universities is the result of neo-liberal policies and the failure of the right wing of the ALP to stand up to that trend. Australian universities in Whitlam's time were free. To gain access a student had to have the requisite minimum HSC results. By the late eighties HECS was introduced as a reluctant acceptance of neo-liberal ideology. The next phase saw the growing commercialisation of universities, in fact de facto part-privatisation, with Vice-Chancellors acting more as business operators, while some of them being paid excessive salary packages. Tertiary education became the third largest export earner while the percentage of casual staff steadily grew, as for instance at Wollongong university, with 75%. Can we go back to what a university is supposed to be? A place of higher learning and research, where the majority of staff is highly qualified and employed with tenure, so that they can speak up fearlessly on matters of great importance to the community, popular or not. It is definitely not a business.

The way back is important and urgent but the foreign students who have paid for and are half-way a course now should not suffer. Most like to be studying in Australia and there are advantages to all parties but a complete revaluation of the practice is certainly called for.

Judith White in John Menadue *"Pearls and Irritations"* (June 11.6.20) made the following comments:

"The university as an institution basic to civil society has two purposes: original research, and the training of young minds; and the two must go hand in hand. Teaching methods are supposed to be based on the Socratic techniques of challenging assumptions and asking questions, with lectures by leading researchers, and tutorials enabling students to engage directly with highly qualified mentors. A healthy campus has a lively cultural life – a dramatic society that attracts mathematicians as well as literature students, a debating club open to students from all disciplines. It's an education that produces the kind of well-rounded minds that have served Australia so well in the past.

The experience of most students today is far removed from that ideal. Young friends tell me of tutorial groups larger in number than the average primary class; of lecture halls filled with overseas students struggling to follow by running translation programs on their laptops; of campuses where most of their peers call in only for a lecture, then have to rush off to casual jobs in order to earn a crust. And that's largely the middle-class students. For working-class kids, faced with the prospect of massive HECS debts, it's a lot harder to get in than it was almost 50 years ago, when the Whitlam government opened up free university education.

After decades of neo-liberalism, universities are being turned into businesses. Vice-Chancellors operate as CEOs on vastly inflated salaries, with University of Sydney VC Michael Spence on upwards of $1.5 million. (An honourable exception is ANU VC, Nobel Prize-winning Professor Brian Schmidt, who requested a 25% pay cut when he signed up in 2016; he's a man with a vision for education that's all too rare these days).

Meanwhile, teaching staff are casualised and either given crushing workloads or left without enough hours to make a living. Wollongong University staff have just been forced into accepting a pay cut of 5-10% as an alternative to further job losses. Experts have long been warning about the consequences of under-funding, especially since the Turnbull government cut funds by $2.2 billion in 2017. Apparently, we can afford $50 billion for obsolete submarines, but only $17 billion for the entire university sector. Under pressure the Group of Eight major universities, led by their well-paid Vice-Chancellors, are looking at a "Research Roadmap to Recovery". Sydney's Michael Spence said that without the return of overseas student in previous numbers it's "all over red rover and it gets really ugly" for research budgets. The alternatives the Group is examining include mergers and that has set alarm bells ringing for Universities Australia and the Regional Universities Network, which fear losing research facilities at smaller institutions.

Australia is already well down the road of corporatising universities on the American model. The century-long undermining of liberal education there was documented by Frank Donoghue in his 2008 book *The Last Professors: The Corporate University and the Fate of the Humanities.* Of business interests he wrote: "Their distrust of the ideal of intellectual inquiry for its own sake led them to insist that if universities were to be preserved at all, they must operate on a different set of principles from those governing the liberal arts."

These are the serious consequences of inappropriate policies based on neo-liberalist ideology. The current position could be difficult to adjust to what the university's purpose and experience should be. Apart from the consequences of the Coronavirus pandemic, diplomatic tensions with the republic of China are factors that could reduce the flow of Chinese students significantly – currently about 40% of the total of overseas students. Australia needs much more competence in Government to be able to change the direction of tertiary education. The rescue of the universities will have to start from that basis.

Tertiary education should be free for our own young citizens. We can continue to invite competent foreign students **at a reasonable fee** but accept and pass only those who genuinely deserve to gain degrees. While it may be difficult to generalise, the positions taken by Judith White there is no other way to restore confidence in our universities than to return to their essential character and purpose. To read in a recent report that Sydney University is contemplating cutting history subjects about the making of the US, slavery, fascism and anti-fascism due to budget-saving measures, is almost unbelievable. We have just witnessed massive global protests about such issues. These proposed cuts were presented as imposed Coronavirus austerity measures, according to Head of History Department, Professor Mark McKenna.

These are the consequences of conservative politicians introducing HECS – a system essentially based on neo-liberal philosophy and not effectively countered by the right-wing on the ALP when in power in the 1980s and 1990s. Some have described the university boom as a gold rush. But despite of having 7 of them in the top 100 in the world, measured by research output only though, the majority now seem financially in trouble. That is not all, the quality of many of them appears to be in serious doubt. Which political party will present the way out, a return to a quality system of higher education? Does the premature ending of the CAE system still make sense now? I would think not!

c. The failure to effectively deal with the responsibility of climate change as a major threat to Australia's future.

This text will not detail criticism of the current Government in respect of their environmental policies. Men and women of science have made that case many times, however the current government has failed to act on their advice in several ways. It has been argued that at least 10 years have been wasted. The most critical failure came when the NEG agreement, put together by Malcolm Turnbull and Josh Frydenberg, was knocked back by the Coalition's Party room when Turnbull was Prime Minister. This was the prelude to the coup that ended his Prime Ministership. This development fully illustrates the vicious circle of Australian politics in that the dominant faction of a major party rules the country from a de facto minority position. In this case the Coalition's party room eventually refused to accept the National Energy Guarantee meritorious proposal, that included a combination of measures and an acceptance of climate change realities. It also indicated a refusal of putting the proposal to a free vote which would mean a joint vote with the ALP. It is a very obvious failure of the two-party adversarial system and, therefore, of the electoral system that has produced it. Turnbull fully explained the treatment of the issue in his recent book. However, he does not relate it to the failure of the system. This is of course in itself a problem, but a separate one.

There had been much discussion in the Coalition about the reliability of alternative energy sources during 2017 and finally Josh Frydenberg had come up with a draft National Energy Guarantee (NEG). The energy Security Board own modelling found that under the NEG:

"an additional 1986 MW of dispatchable capacity would be built over and above the 2000 MW of Snowy 2.0. The NEG, however, was technology-agnostic and the reliability requirement didn't discriminate between coal, gas, hydro or even batteries. All could provide firm, reliable, on-demand power and it was up to the market to get the right mix. Obviously, given the need to reduce emissions over time, a combination of renewables plus storage was attractive, and the most likely, way of providing new dispatchable capacity." (p. 613)

There were further major advantages:

"The ESB found the NEG would result in a reduction in the wholesale electricity prices by 23 percent between 2020 and 2030. Together with our other policies, that would mean household bills would be about $400 a year less compared to bills in 2017. For business it meant a lot. A supermarket would save about $400,000" (p. 613)

According to Turnbull there had never been an energy policy with a broader base of support than the NEG. The only source of opposition remained within the Liberal and National parties. Figure that! But it had majority support in the Coalition Party room initially, despite some opposition predominantly coming from Tony Abbott; later eight had said "they would cross the floor". The question for Turnbull was, in the course of 2018, how many of our colleagues would vote against the NEG proposal? Significantly, there was in fact further and much wider support for it as well, in the community:

"the NEG won support from the business community, the energy sector, the trade union movement, and, most importantly, the state governments, who are members of the COAG Energy Council. Even the Labor ones responded positively. Business, above all, was relieved that at last there appeared to be a durable energy policy that dealt with emission reductions and reliability in the energy sector. It was a framework that would enable firms to invest with confidence" (p. 614)

But the support in the Coalition Party room began to crumble and this had probably much to do with an attempt to topple Australia's Prime Minister. Nevertheless, the nature of the decision-making process then shifted to whether or not the plan should be put to the Parliament as a whole in a free vote. Turnbull's instinct was to do just that, he wrote, but the "Cabinet was vehemently opposed to this". The rest is history, because failure to do just that, which almost certainly would have been successful, resulted in the coup that toppled the Prime Minister.

One has to say then that the Westminster practice of Cabinet solidarity played a role here, with negative consequences. However, what is particularly relevant is that a majority decision on the NEG, a positive long overdue plan, did not materialise as the result of a negative attitude of a maximum of twelve Coalition MPs. **What it meant was that 139 of the 151 MPs did not have the chance to approve the NEG plan.** What it also meant was, for Turnbull, that he was removed as PM shortly afterwards. Turnbull could and should have asserted his authority over his party and the Parliament as a whole. Almost certainly the legislation would have been passed into law, a major victory. He was behind in the polls, but his position would have been strengthened altogether had he not acted in the way the Westminster practice apparently required. The end result was that this system totally failed Australia's national interest in that the saga ended without an effective climate change policy; in addition, a very competent PM would be removed shortly after in a coup by a minority of the people's representatives.

Summing up in conclusion, these are major system failures that can and need to be avoided in future. Australia is now still left without effective climate change policies. The Morrison Government does not understand the need to take this on.

CHAPTER 7

WHO SETS THE NATIONAL POLITICAL AGENDAS IN AUSTRALIA? WHO REALLY ARE OUR REPRESENTATIVES?

Distrust in the system has been established. Why is it so?

The remedy is system change!

The gradual decline in trust of politicians and the political system has been competently established by academics of the University of Canberra in 2018. They are: Professor Mark Evans, Max Halupka and Gerry Stoker of the Institute for Governance and Policy Analysis. The result of their research is explained in a document " Trust and Democracy in Australia".

An abstract of the document is reproduced here followed by a short discussion of further aspects pertaining to it:

Abstract

"Australians should rightly be proud of their hard-won democratic traditions and freedoms, and the achievement of stable government which has delivered social and economic wellbeing for the country's citizens. However, the findings presented in this chapter should give all democrats pause for thought. We find compelling evidence of an increasing trust divide between government and citizens reflected in the decline of democratic satisfaction; receding trust in politicians, political parties and other key institutions (especially media); and a lack of public confidence in the capacity of government to address public policy concerns. Australia is currently experiencing a culture shift from an allegiant to a divergent democratic culture (Dalton & Welzel 2014), with an increasing number of citizens searching for a new politics to represent their values and defend their material needs and aspirations for the future. This chapter draws on data derived from a national survey of 1021 Australians in July 2018 that sought to explore the relationship between trust in the political system and attitudes towards democracy. We understand political trust as a relational concept that is about 'keeping promises and agreements' (Hetherington 20015: 1). This is in keeping with the Organisation for Economic Co-operation and Development's definition of trust as 'holding a positive perception about the actions of an individual or an organization' (OECD 2017: 16). The survey questions were designed by the authors and included some questions that previously had been asked of similar samples in 2014 and 2016, allowing for time series analysis (see Evans, Halupka & Stoker 2014; Evans & Stoker 2016; Stoker et al. 2017)."

The researchers found that "Australians' trust in politicians and democracy was at an all-time low". They also established that a majority of citizens were highly critical of the continuous conflict in the federal Parliament. These views were developed over a four-year period – up to July 2018. A good deal more bad news was to follow!

"Our latest research, conducted in July 2018 (**prior** to the Liberal Party's leadership spill), includes a quantitative survey of a representative sample of 20 focus groups and 1,021 Australians from a wide range of demographic backgrounds. We understood political trust in this survey as "keeping promises and agreements".

Democratic decline and renewal

When asked to select three aspects of Australian democracy that they liked the most, the top three in 2018 were (in order):

1. "Australia has been able to provide good education, health, welfare and other public services to its citizens"

2. "Australia has experienced a good economy and lifestyle"

3. "Australian elections are free and fair".

Respondents were least likely to choose features that praised (or showed engagement) with current democratic politics. The findings suggest that Australians are happy with the underlying democratic infrastructure of Australian society that allows them to achieve a high standard of living but are less positive or engaged about day-to-day political operations.

Australians are deeply unhappy with democratic politics

"Fewer than 41% of Australian citizens are satisfied with the way democracy works in Australia, down from 86% in 2007. Public satisfaction has fallen particularly sharply since 2013, when 72% of Australian citizens were satisfied. Generation X is least satisfied (31%) and the Baby Boomers most satisfied (50%)."

Read more: Why do Australians hate politics?

"Just 31% of the population trust federal government. State and local governments perform little better, with just over a third of people trusting them. Ministers and MPs (whether federal or state) rate at just 21%, while more than 60% of Australians believe the honesty and integrity of politicians is very low."

The three biggest grievances people have with politicians are:

1. "they are not accountable for broken promises
2. "they don't deal with the issues that really matter
3. "big business has too much power (Liberal and National Party voters identify trade unions instead of big business).

The continued decline of political trust has also contaminated public confidence in other key political institutions. Only five rate above 50% – police, military, civic well-being organisations (such as Headspace or community services), universities and healthcare institutions.

Trust was lowest in political parties (16%) and web-based media (20%). Trust in banks and web-based media has significantly decreased since the last survey. This reflects the impact of the Banking Royal Commission and the Facebook-Cambridge Analytica data scandal."

However: the researchers also found that the desire for democratic reform is "extremely strong".

"Our survey revealed a significant appetite for reform. Nine out of 15 proposed reforms received net agreement rates above 50%." The top five reforms favoured in the survey were:

1. "limiting money donated to parties and spent in elections
2. "the right for voters to recall ineffective local MPs
3. "giving all MPs a free vote in parliament
4. "co-designing policies with ordinary Australians
5. "citizen juries to solve complex problems that parliament can't fix.

"Reforms aimed at improving the practice of representative politics were the most popular, followed by reforms aimed at giving citizens a greater say. There was also strong support for reforms aimed at creating a stronger community or local focus to decision-making. Only reforms aimed at guaranteeing the representation of certain groups failed to attract majority support.

"Remarkably, accessing more detailed information about innovative reforms led to greater support for those reforms. This is an important finding, revealing the importance of strategic communication in winning the war of ideas."

We are at the tipping points

"Liberal democracies are founded on a delicate balance between trust and distrust. Our survey findings suggest we may have reached a tipping point due to a deepening trust divide in Australia, which has increased **in scope and intensity since 2007.**"

This is certainly important research but the question "Why is it so?" is only partly answered by respondents it seems and the remedies suggested are quite limited. They do not relate to specific governance system change and this may be, *in part at least*, because the existing systems seem to have worked reasonably well in the past. However, an electoral system like Proportional Representation – Party List would fit the broad preferences, as well as considerably more emphasis on stronger Local Government!

It is interesting and educational for the visiting public that the Museum of Democracy in Canberra (Old Parliament House) has displayed key aspects of the research finding in the Museum. It would be good if the Museum would now also engage in discussion and displays that would recommend alternative governance systems!

Can the Murdoch Media Empire (Newscorp) be blamed as the culprit?

Former PM Malcom Turnbull devotes considerable attention to this question in his recent book; he certainly tends to the view that Newscorp wanted him out. There is some truth in that but, understandably, the claim seems coloured by very personal adverse experiences. However, it may well have applied to the Government under Tony Abbott and his supporters, as Turnbull argues. The important reality is that external forces, like Newscorp, have a much greater impact if they can manipulate a conservative faction of one major party (in a two-party system) than a coalition of parties forming a majority government (in a multi-party system). Nevertheless, the claimed destabilisation of Turnbull, as PM, by Newscorp, rather than by Murdoch personally, apparently with a view to returning Abbott to the Prime Ministership, appears credible. Even if the 2019 election had been lost by the Coalition, which looked likely, a comeback of Tony Abbot was being planned. The fear of an ALP win under Bill Shorten, which looked a near-certainty at the time, appears to have generated this plotting by the conservative faction of the Liberal Party. The role of Newscorp and involvement of Murdoch himself could actually have resulted in a Dutton Government in spite of the fact that Turnbull consistently had more personal support as a leader, when compared to Shorten, among voters.

One has to say therefore that the involvement of Newscorp, and also the late-night radio station Sky News, led by Abbott's associate Peta Credlin, was extensive and destabilising the Turnbull Government. In the main, it ran counter to the consistent majority support of the voters for the ALP in the forthcoming 2019 election. Undoubtedly, this drama also further reduced the trust of the voters in Australia's political system. Again, the composition of a legislature, comprised of two major parties, both of which comprise two factions, provides the potential for minority government. Such an undemocratic outcome clearly is the result of the current electoral system.

Further views on renewal in Australia – What about the growing power of lobbyists. What about "Sortition"?

So, let's explore the question further: **Why is it so?** Some argue, as did Paul Sheehan earlier in the SMH that, in NSW at least, staffers have taken over as candidates for political office, and lobbyists which he calls the Concierge Factions, dominate the NSW Government. That may be part of the explanation but there are several other aspects to this question really.

> "The NSW Liberal Party is now in the grip of the "concierge faction": the lobbyists, the facilitators, the door-openers. These are the career staffers, career party machinists, members of lobbying firms and corporate lobbyists who go into politics to monetise political access." (SMH, 24.1.16).

Another journalist, Judith Ireland has written about lobbying and lobbyist in Canberra at some length (SMH, 12.10.'19).

> "Senator Jacqui Lambie has called them 'backstage passes of the lobbying class'" They are the bright orange-coloured plastic passes worn by the lobbyists who descend on Canberra during sitting weeks. The lobbyists represent interests big and small, left and right and everything in between. But they all have one mission: to influence politics. Hundreds of millions of dollars are spent each year by their clients in a bid to be heard in the corridors and offices of Parliament House. What is this lobbying class? Who is in it? What do they actually do? And what are the potential pitfalls for the rest of us, whose influence on politics usually extends to voting every three years?

What really is lobbying?

"Lobbying is communication in an effort to influence government decision-making", according to the federal government's lobbyist register.

Lobbyists are employed by clients – from ASX100 companies to small not-for-profits – to talk to the government on their behalf. This might mean seeking face-to-face meetings with politicians, calling their staff or speaking to journalists and senior public servants. While the meetings often take place in the office suites of Parliament House or the restaurants of Canberra's Civic and Kingston foreshores during sitting weeks, lobbyists are also easily spotted among the tables at Aussies Cafe at Parliament. Lobbyists will be engaged for a whole range of reasons. A group or business may just want to have a relationship with and "be known" to the government. They may have a particular problem with a bill or a policy that affects their business or interests. Or they may want their point of view heard as a policy is developed. One lobbyist described their job as "translation": they understand how politics, Parliament and Canberra work, they know who to speak to and can use those skills to try and solve a problem for their client. This specialist knowledge includes the complexity of federal-state relations (who is responsible for what), the role of public servants, what power ministerial staffers have, how legislation works and where different MPs are likely to line up on different issues.

What are the criticisms of the lobbying system?

The lobbyist register describes lobbying as a "legitimate activity and an important part of the democratic process". "Lobbyists can help individuals and organisations communicate their views ... and, in doing so, improve outcomes for the individual and the community as a whole." But there are several major criticisms of the system. One being that the lobbying register doesn't have to include all the people who are actually lobbying. Many political analysts also express deep misgivings about how the system works, pointing to the "revolving door" between working in government and working in influential industries such as food, gambling and alcohol.

117

The Greens want information about meetings with lobbyists published and a five year "cooling-off" period during which ministers and senior staff can't be engaged in private enterprise that raises a conflict of interest or benefit for their past role and connections. The Grattan Institute (Melbourne) similarly wants ministerial diaries to be published and has called for the lobbyist register to be linked to the orange passes. Senator Lambie also supports the five-year cooling-off period and wants the lobbying code of conduct to apply to anyone who lobbies, regardless of whether they are on the register. She says this should be policed by the Australian Competition and Consumer Commission.

How many lobbyists visit Parliament? As of October, there are 884 lobbyists on the federal lobbyist register, from 279 firms, lobbying on behalf of 3691 clients. There are 227 Members of Parliament. But many people who lobby in Canberra are not required to register as lobbyists. These include charities and religious organisations, not-for-profits, people making representations on behalf of family or friends, or those people engaging in lobbying on their own behalf. This means unions, or big companies who have in-house lobbyists, do not need to register. People who have worked in state politics also do not have to register on the federal list. A good – although not perfect – indication of how many people actually lobby is the number of "sponsored" or orange pass holders to Parliament: there are 2380. There is a total of 12,000 passes issued across various categories in. These are unescorted passes to the private areas of Parliament House, valid for the term of Parliament. To get one, you have to be sponsored by an MP or senator who has known you for at least 12 months. You need to pass a police check and you need to have "a regular and significant business requirement for unescorted access".

The Department of Parliamentary Services notes that some orange pass holders are not lobbyists but others with a legitimate claim to visit Parliament, such as MP's family members. (Public servants, ministerial advisers and other staff who come to Parliament wear a different-coloured pass and would not be on the orange pass list). But the orange pass list is not made public. Parliamentary staff have previously said it would be a security risk to publish it, as people could steal passes or pretend, they were a pass holder. Britain and New Zealand are among countries that have published lists of pass holders.

Given the growth of consultants one may well ask what has happened to our professional public services?

The development of effective, professional, independent and impartial public services in Western countries dated back to the second half of the 19th century. Some would say that the US took the lead in this, around the 1860s, but it soon spread to European countries together with the growth of political parties and democracy. These developments were further advanced in the 20th century and ensured that elected Governments could rely on specialist administrators providing impartial advice to the peoples representatives of political parties, whatever their particular preferences. At times these public servants may have become political players as well as was characterised in the famous *Yes Minister* & *Yes Prime Minister* TV programs.

In Australia, certainly the federal mandarins were significant administrators in the post-war era, and several have become well-known as for instance "Nugget" Coombs, who was Head of the Reserve Bank for many years in the 1960s. With the growth of neo-liberalism, from the 1980s onwards, the expansion of private lobbyists seems to have been accompanied by the shrinking of public services. Conservative Governments have tended to reduce the number of public servants while connections with consultants have been stimulated. The operation of the class and cultural wars in Australia, a by-product of the two-party system, has accentuated these divisions. In a new Australia, post-Covid-19, a better balance of diverse interest should be achievable. There can be little doubt that the traditional adversarial political system is the very cause of these counterproductive divisions. A more balanced, diverse representation, that is certainly achievable, would benefit Australia.

The current distrust of the politicians, as the political class, together with the failure to achieve governance system change, has also resulted in a few proposals for the renewal of the democracy which may be far-reaching but are relatively untested. Compared to what is suggested in this text they are idealistic. They are in part directly related to the poor performance of politicians and the political class in a number of Western democracies, including the UK, as well as Australia.

It may be appropriate and helpful that these advocacies are mentioned and briefly discussed here, to assess their credibility or part-credibility and achievability. E.g., four theorists were discussed in an article by Luke Slattery in the SMH's *Good Weekend* (23.6.2016) under the title *"Silver tail subversives: the men aiming to change a system in which they prosper".* Another recent text which deals with that very issue even more directly and comprehensively is Brett Hennig's *The End of Politicians – Time for a Real Democracy*, Unbound, 2017.

Of the four interviewed by journalist Slattery three are men of independent means who have promoted and financed voluntary organisations pursuing alternative democratic ideals. The fourth one, Richard Walsh is a well-known former 1970s activist, of modest means, who has published a book *Reboot – Democracy make-over to empower Australian voters*, MUP, 2017. Walsh writes: *"If you want real change, change the system."* Bravo! He proposes several solutions, some obviously reasonable (and long overdue), others more speculative and/or utopian; some are missing perhaps but his is a short book. First up, for him as well, is Australia's electoral system, which, in seven of our nine lower houses, is based on individual Single Member Districts (SMDs). Walsh is attracted to the Hare-Clark proportional representation system, more especially to the original ideas of the Englishman Thomas Hare, who lived in the mid-19th century. This system was partly applied in Tasmania; first in 1896 and later, in 1907, extending it to five districts of six members; later also in the ACT. The multi-member district base of the system has undoubtedly great advantages. It results in a much more cooperative (non-adversarial) culture but Walsh omits to mention that later adaptations of Hare-Clark in Australia have resulted in several problems, especially in the Senate. He does refer encouragingly to the introduction of a form of PR party list system in New Zealand (MMP, two votes), which he recommends for Australia. Strangely, there is no mention at all of the much more widely used PR – Party List systems in many non-English-speaking countries – no less than 89 of them – whereby voters have a wide choice but only one vote.

A further recommendation is the abolition of the Senate which would of course require a far-reaching amendment to the Australia's federal Constitution, really a re-write. As a Republican Walsh says Australia needs a new President and this official should be popularly elected (from six candidates) as well as a 12-person elected Council to assist him/her, elected from 20 candidates by preferential vote. The President would have a largely symbolic role. As to the new House of Representatives Walsh recommends two categories of MPs: those elected by "open" and those by "closed" electors.

The other three authors discussed are Transfield Holdings managing director and New Democracy Foundation head Luca Belgiorno-Nettis; Melbourne property developer and publisher Morry Schwartz; and Sydney venture capitalist Mark Carnegie. Slattery describes: "They are the silver tail subversives determined to shake up a moribund political culture. Their prestige in the corporate and cultural worlds insulates them from charges of left-wing ratbaggery but leaves them vulnerable to blue-collar scorn and the scepticism of a tall-poppy-scything society innately hostile towards intellectual elites. Or elites, full stop. Something unforeseen has happened to Western democracy in the early decades of the 21st century, and professors and pundits around the globe are struggling to make sense of it. Seven years after the empty democratic promises of the Arab Spring, a bleak Occidental Autumn has settled over the landscape. "Populism is on the rise. And the political class – statesmanship itself – is on the nose". The future of mainstream politics may depend on its capacity for renewal and reform, a point both Walsh and Luca Belgiorno-Nettis are keen to drive home. Belgiorno-Nettis referred to a national survey done by *New Democracy*, in March 2017, in which 81% felt that "everyday people should play a bigger part in government decisions that affect their lives". The big reform suggested is citizen juries of randomly selected people who will be asked to debate, deliberate and recommend policy to arms of government. He referred to Athenian Assembly in Greece as an earlier example in fifth century BC and provides the technical name *Sortition* for this system.

Athens was a small city state where about one third of the citizens had the vote, excluding women, the slaves and the many foreigners. Apparently, there are no comparable examples in the world of the 19th and 20th century. However, there are some limited examples of randomly selected citizen assemblies in several countries dealing with specific, delegated decision-making processes on particular issues, including financial and tax issues.

Morry Schwartz, a well-known publisher, starting with *Outback Press* in the Whitlam area, later, for example, *The Quarterly Essay*, The *Monthly* and *The Saturday Paper.* He is a democrat and a Republican and reportedly said, "we don't need wholesale changes, but we do need an Australian President". That is quite surprising given the highly progressive nature of his publications.

It is fear that motivates Mark Carnegie to speak out publicly on troubles to which most people of his kind, enjoying the view from the first-class lounge and the marina, are inured. "Fear for my kids", he explained.

He speaks regularly at conferences and in the media. His ideal Australia is a more equal Australia. It's not, though, a levelling instinct that drives him; more a case of broadening the opportunities to rise. The alternative to greater equality of opportunity, he insists, is "leaving a whole lot of social potential on the scrapheap".

Like Walsh and Belgiorno-Nettis, Carnegie is frustrated by the political culture, particularly the chokehold of political parties on ideas – he calls it "vote politics". But he has no whiz-bang structural reform to promote. In fact, he's not so much concerned with the structure of government as society: social capital – the economist's term for the social fabric – is one of his big themes.

Finally, this bring us to the informative new text by English writer Brett Hennig (2017) *The End of Politicians – Time for a Real Democracy*, Unbound. Much of this book is devoted to the philosophy of developing a true democracy rather than improving a "representative democracy".

That concept is considered as "a contradiction in terms" because the representatives are failing in their duty to represent the people who voted them in. But in other parts the randomly selected citizen assemblies are also presented as a new, or further, "mutation" of democracy. In later chapters examples of stratified randomly selected, citizen assemblies for limited or local government purposes are provided. According to Professor Erik Olin Wright, author of **Envisioning Real Utopias,** the Hennig book "provides a powerful critique of the democratic deficits in all forms of electoral democracy". This is not quite correct. In fact, the book of 18 chapters, deals primarily with the electoral systems of the UK, the US and Australia and finds them rightly deficient in many respects, especially in terms of democratic representation. Their elections are largely based on the single-member-district (SMD) system that originated in Britain and was exported to the US and Australia, and to some other English-speaking countries as well (e.g., South Africa, **where it greatly contributed to the emergence of Apartheid from 1948 onwards**). There are many references to well-known authors on the subject most of whom also originate from these three countries. There are graphs and statistics covering several democracies, or pseudo-democracies, in the world, and of trends such as the, to the author, unexpected survival and strong growth of democracies after WWII. There are also some references to other electoral systems in other countries which throw up important unanswered questions: "In plurality-majority voting systems, such as that of the UK, one candidate is elected from each area, resulting in a parliament typically dominated by two leading parties. In such systems equality refers to an equality of initial opportunity to vote."

In proportional voting systems, as used, for example in the Netherlands, multiple politicians are usually elected from extended areas in proportion to the votes gained (which often results in many parliamentary parties, and hence coalition governments). The quality in proportional systems refers to the equality of influence on the outcome. In both systems, each vote has an equal value in theory, although in plurality-majority systems it is obvious that many more votes have no value in practice, as they will not contribute to the composition of parliament. "The analysis of the political inequality of certain votes could go even further: election results in a UK-type system often hinge on the outcome of a handful of marginal seats, so the choices of swinging voters may be crucial, making their votes very powerful indeed." (Hennig, p. 17)

Some of the great contributions of the Dutch-American Professor Arend Lijphart are mentioned in Hennig's book although Lijphart's very relevant work is not listed in his Select Biography. As the proposed remedy by the **Sortition Foundation** to the current political malaise in the three countries may gain some support, despite acknowledged huge practical problems, this description in the Hennig book clearly provides a significantly different alternative:

"Proportional representation systems are an alternative that leads to many more parties attracting votes and obtaining parliamentary seats". He compares the percentage of seats that the three major parties or coalitions received in recent national elections to the legislative house of parliaments in the UK, Australia, Germany and the Netherlands. Wherever one comes across the question of plurality-majority versus proportional electoral systems, the latter – used for example, in the Netherlands – is more representative of the people's votes than the former, as used in the UK. We should also reflect on the outcomes of recent general elections in Britain where both Conservative PM David Cameron and the new Conservative PM Boris Johnson were elected on minority votes. The US journalist Amanda Taub demonstrated recently in the *New York Times* that Johnson would not have been elected if the election had been conducted on the basis of proportional representation – party list.

CHAPTER 8

AUSTRALIA NEEDS A NEW CONSTITUTION

There are many reasons why the Constitution needs to be rewritten completely. An important question is: how can that process be started?

The Australian Law Reform Commission is to be congratulated on starting a new broad-ranging Inquiry on Law Reform in Australia. Not surprisingly it was established in 1975, an explosive year in which the shortcomings of the Australian Constitution were first discussed at great length. These issues basically have remained unresolved ever since. Really, the situation has further deteriorated. In its introductory paper of 15 May 2019, the Commission reiterated that state of affairs which, at the first public meeting at the UNSW was described as "depressive" and suggested that only a rewrite would do. It is now imperative not only to remedy the deplorable situation but even more to provide Australia with a modern basic set of rules worthy of its growing multicultural, democratic society. In 2018 Australia had the Section 44 drama to contend with, not actually the first time, resulting in no less than 15 costly by-elections. In addition, the refusal to accept the Uluru Statement of the Heart recommendations by the Indigenous peoples of Australia by PM Turnbull, on account of being "too problematic for a referendum", is indicative o dangerous stagnation. In 2019 the lack of a Bill of Rights, again, generated complex public arguments about the freedom of the press and free speech. The fact of the matter is that the archaic Australian Constitution regularly confronts this society. Piecemeal tinkering, having proved ineffectual for many years, is no longer an option. Surely the time has come for a much more drastic approach. The

Commission will look at several law areas, starting with, significantly, the Australian Constitution. I attended its first public meeting held in the Law School of the University of NSW early last year and presented them with a copy of my self-published book "*YES, we can.....rewrite the Australian Constitution*", BookPod, Melbourne.

Most Australians do not know much about the Australian Constitution. Given the relatively peaceful society, steady economic growth since WWII, a large non-Anglo migrant population and lack of easy to understand information, this is not so surprising. A generalised view has taken root, that "the Constitution has served Australia well" or "it cannot be so bad that it needs to be overhauled completely". There is also a view that "Australians are conservative and therefore would not be keen to change the Constitution or governance systems." Some Prime Ministers keep saying that. Frankly, that may apply to a very small minority only. What is true is that ignorance about the Constitution and political processes and governance systems is widespread. In recent years distrust of politicians and the political system has increased dramatically. But then there are also those Australians who are quite familiar with the Constitution, know that much of the document is outdated, but believe, are convinced even, that major change is extremely difficult. And then, on top of that, there are certainly several scholars and journalists who have tried very hard to present alternatives, regrettably, thus far, all in vain. But the connection between the Constitution and, more generally, other governance systems and the lack of confidence in the politicians is not always understood.

It would be a major improvement in Australia's democracy if there was a new Constitution of which the overwhelming majority would be proud. Few people would disagree with that. This is the time that progressive politicians should come forward and say that! This is the time that we can put an end the people's ignorance of the Constitution by starting to work on a document that every Australian, young and old, is familiar with, has had some input in the making of it. If we are to have a Republic let the campaign coincide with the preparation of a new Constitution. Quite frankly, that seems to be entirely desirable, useful and logical.

The failure of the 1999 Referendum to establish a Republic was an event that generated a number of crash courses and ad hoc bodies meant to rapidly generate knowledge about the Constitution and constitutional issues. These had long been inadequately covered by universities and high schools. Sadly, it proved to be unsuccessful. A worthwhile public Senate Inquiry into causes of the failure of the Referendum, in 2005, established conclusively that the lack of education about governance system issues was a major limiting factor in the 1990s. However, it needs to be said that the machinations of the Howard Government, favouring a symbolic President selected by politicians only, also did not help in 1999. No less than 16% of those who favoured a Republic but voted against the proposal, did so on account of this aspect of the Referendum proposal.

There are undoubtedly serious problems with the Australian Constitution and the question now should be: with what kind of Constitutional framework should Australians approach the issue of the Republic next time? Is it conceivable that these two ambitions could be rolled into one? It is not only the structure of the national state, the many vital issues not covered in 1901, as well as the separation from the British monarchy that are at stake. Social, economic, political and, perhaps especially, environmental changes, require to be expressed in a meaningful new Constitution. In particular, the electoral system as well as effective rural and regional development, have made a meaningful rewrite essential. Gender issues, multiculturalism and the special place of the First Nation of course should be included. The protection of both political and economic sovereignty of Australia needs to be spelled out so that foreign ownership is properly regulated.

The political system has been in real turmoil, followed by major other upheavals. Prime Ministers come and go. High expectations of the previous Prime Minister, Malcolm Turnbull, proved misguided. How could this staunch Republican, who chaired the Australian Republic Movement, be muzzled by the conservative faction of his Party? Why was he unable to effectively appeal to the middle ground of Australian politics? Australia is now governed by the conservative factions of the Liberal and National Parties' Coalition. Clearly, just a change to a Republic would not change this situation. Not at all. The current Prime Minister, Scott Morrison was a surprise winner in the May 2019 federal election. The Republic issue and any other Constitutional change issues have moved into the background, for the moment. Morrison's performance, until the outbreak of the Coronavirus crisis, had not impressed Australians, especially during the recent severe fires in four states, which, initially, he regarded as a state issue rather than a national (federal) concern.

We can establish that, quite apart from the conservatism of the major parties, there are three factors specifically which have prevented the updating of the colonial Constitution:

1. Clause 128, requiring a national majority as well as a majority in a majority of states (four out of six), a condition the smaller states demanded in the 1890s.

2. The adversarial two-party system itself – a direct result of the electoral system.

3. The constitutional requirement that only federal politicians can propose federal constitutional amendments.

Nevertheless, one outstanding, courageous and somewhat unexpected judgement came from the High Court in 1992 when it decided, by a majority of 6 :1 in the Eddie Mabo case, that the concept of Terra Nullius was wrong, and that Indigenous people could claim land rights if continued prior occupancy could be established. Clearly, Australia was not an empty country when the British claimed New South Wales in 1770, as was apparently assumed or the Indigenous people were not considered as citizens in any European sense. However, the Indigenous people had lived here for a very long time, possibly for 65,000 years. At least that erroneous doctrine was removed, but this judgement did not amend the Constitution in relation to Sections that concern the Indigenous people (Sections 25 and 51xxvi). These have been the subject of much recent controversy and discussion. New constitutional proposals, the Uluru Statement of the Heart, were developed by the First Nation. Regrettably, these were soon rejected by the Turnbull Government. While the struggle to take this to a referendum continues an entirely new Constitution which includes the Indigenous Voice surely is preferable.

To date only 8 of 44 amendment proposals have been successful. The number of possible and desirable proposals is greater, probably much greater than 44, but the fear of failure is such that only very likely successful proposals, supported by both major parties, are put to the voters. No Government likes to risk failure of a costly Referendum unless a promise made in an election campaign of course, as John Howard did in the 1996 election and was elected. Regrettably, the actual proposal he put forward had little chance of being approved and failed.

Therefore, further piecemeal tinkering clearly makes no sense. There is a new preparedness in Australia, following the Coronavirus crisis that has shaken the nation and fostered a new sense of unity, to consider major reforms. Given the current state of Australia's political system at least two measures need to be considered.

1. A complete rewrite of the Australian Constitution need to be undertaken as soon as possible following a genuinely Independent Inquiry. Serving politicians should not be members of the Commission of Constitutional Renewal. Obviously, still really useful, uncontroversial sections of the existing Constitution can be left in the new draft but much else of it should go or be replaced. The notion that Australia needs to remain in the Westminster mould for some reason, while some practices are clearly counterproductive, is questionable. This should not be the basis of new proposals.

2. It would help if the Governor-General adopted an active and innovative role to start this process. The existing **written** Constitution actually provides for this possibility. In spite of the fact that in the Westminster system the Governor-General has a largely symbolic role, as a principal advisor to the Queen (of Australia), this person has sufficient executive capacity to intervene – on the basis of the "Reserve Powers" in any case, whatever the constitutional conventions. This is especially so as

it is likely now that neither major party acting alone is able to achieve constitutional reform! They have had three decades to act. Some would say really since 1975. So, where to from here? Another century of ineffectual piecemeal tinkering? Grow up Australia! A Republic with a brand-new Constitution is the real answer here.

The recommendation of opting for a complete rewrite of the Constitution may concern some people, especially in a period of high unemployment as is fully expected to occur in the post-pandemic period. Some might say this is not the right time even though the case for that position is not strong. Against that view can be said that, apart from abolishing federation, a rewrite of the Constitution can hardly affect employment or the economy for that matter. If anything, it can only benefit the economy in the longer term as duplication of functions should be avoided. Naturally, major changes need to be introduced in stages, according to a generally agreed plan. Abolishing federation, while creating more jobs at the local and regional government levels, would result in the unemployment of some state public servants who cannot be redeployed elsewhere. Such people, naturally, should be fully compensated, an expense that is part of the transition plan. Early retirement is another option for some.

The process should be started by changing the electoral system, as explained in Chapter 2. This will result in a different political culture, different from what Australia has clearly rejected in the last 15 years. Secondly, Governments need to be selected by appointing Ministers from outside the elected legislatures so as to ensure that the quality of Government is enhanced significantly. Proposals for Constitutional renewal will flow from these changes naturally. The trust in the reformed system will return.

CHAPTER 9

THE REAL ISSUE: WHAT KIND OF REPUBLIC?

In late 2016 there was a short-lived revival of the Australian Republican Movement (ARM) when Malcolm Turnbull, its former initiator and Chair, was Prime Minister. The ARM had claimed that a majority in both the lower and upper houses of federal parliament supported Australia becoming a Republic.

The journalist Paul Karp provided the detail of this short-lived hope as follows in *The Guardian, 16.12.16*

> "The Australian Republican Movement is backed by Malcolm Turnbull, and it claims the support of other senior government figures including deputy Liberal leader Julie Bishop, and moderates in cabinet Christopher Pyne, Marise Payne and Simon Birmingham. Even leading younger conservative figures Josh Frydenberg and George Christensen support a republic, although the latter says his support is "'subject to the right model being chosen' including a series of significant and ambitious constitutional changes.
>
> In all, 81 members of the House of Representatives, and 40 members of the Senate have declared their support for an Australian republic, the movement says. According to ARM the number may be even higher as 58 lower house MPs have not stated a position on the republic. Eleven lower house MPs are committed monarchists. In the upper house, 21 senators were undeclared or undecided and 15 favour the monarchy.
>
> ARM hopes the figures will help persuade Turnbull to take the lead on amending the constitution to install an Australian head of state. Turnbull

unsuccessfully led the "yes" campaign in the failed republic referendum in 1999. After becoming prime minister in September 2015, Turnbull said that there will be no move to become a republic until Queen Elizabeth is no longer on the throne."

Turnbull spoke at the ARM's 25th anniversary celebration a few days later. Peter FitzSimons, chairman of the ARM, said Turnbull "has a unique chance to put the republican cause firmly back at the centre of the national agenda. The majority of the public want it. Every premier and chief minister wants it. Now it turns out that our federal representatives agree as well."

The then Labor leader Bill Shorten called on Turnbull to join him and work to make new progress to an Australian Republic. According to ARM's figures, the Greens are the most pro-republic, with 100% in support, followed by Labor (93%). Just 19 Coalition parliamentarians are openly in support of a republic (17%) although most, 65, are undecided or undeclared. George Christensen, chief whip of the Nationals, said: "A renewed push for an Australian republic gives hope ... of having someone who is Australian and not subject to any foreign power as our head of state." He said it also gave hope that "we can reform government to make it more representative and responsive to the needs and desires of the Australian people". Echoing the debates around the 1999 referendum, Christensen would favour a directly elected head of state.

However, in his anniversary speech Turnbull's support for a Republic was very qualified and cautious. He made it clear that the "**ARM has to get the people on side**". Was that not the case then? Not sufficiently. The reality was that the voters were becoming increasingly disenchanted with the political system and that popular support for the Republic had actually declined somewhat. At the time John Hewson again described the political system as a "mire", Australia needed to be rescued from (SMH 16/12/16). Regrettably, Hewson's own recommendations were questionable in that they provide suggestions of major party cooperation of a high order within the traditional adversarial two-party system. This had been virtually completely absent until the recent Coronavirus drama. However, apart from the issues Mr. Turnbull had in mind, mainly economic and budgetary ones, major sleeping issues such as governance system problems, were not mentioned at all by either major party. In 1999 the voters rejected a Politicians' Republic; AND a Politicians' President! So, to gain serious public support the ARM should significantly broaden their Minimalist platform. In fact, the Movement's Minimalism has been a hindrance in the way of its success, actually from its inception. That the Premiers of the States are now in favour of a Minimalist Republic may be a plus for a Minimalist Republic, but this is clearly NOT what the people want. That is what will count! And the people's Republic is not just about a directly elected President either, an absolutely obvious requirement to start off with, but they want the sick political system, the "mire", as Hewson put it, cleaned up. Just what could this involve? This book is about that. Let us go over some crucial aspects that the ARM, specifically, needs to address.

What about replacing the Federation (a very costly and dysfunctional structure), addressing the archaic electoral system, and removing aspects of the Westminster system, which basically guarantee that we end up with far too many amateurs in our Parliaments? Furthermore, why not start a discussion about the frozen Australian Constitution altogether? The ARM, since its inception, has always been concerned to "not frighten the horses" but could it be that was and is a fundamentally erroneous strategy? It could well be very helpful to adopt the role of a non-parliamentary political movement that would soon eclipse our clearly non-reformist major parties. These parties have obviously shied away from considering governance system reform. Each of them, and jointly as the adversarial "two-party system", is part of the problem. One could say they ARE the problem, of stagnation. The ARM, led by the well-known journalist and author Peter FitzSimons, could and should reconsider its role as soon as possible. The ARM's fear of losing popular support appears to be stronger than the expectation of winning additional support. How then could it generate new support?

Australian politics and governance can improve greatly.

The Australian voters are realising that although their political system has become a major problem, in a situation of major danger, cooperation between the major parties is in fact achievable. This is a very important new factor on the road to major reforms because all politicians now realise that reform of the system is indeed at least a possibility.

It is difficult to assess if this can result in a more general desire for renewal of the political system, given the innate conservatism of both major parties. Optimistically, it is conceivable that a third force, conceivably the Senate, can push the major parties to accept that further cooperation, would now be very desirable, even essential.

The broadcasters, of course especially the ABC and SBS, could also play a major role in such a campaign for renewal. Certainly, some individuals and smaller parties, are aware of alternatives, but they usually have insufficient clout and may be unorganized amongst themselves. As argued before, the conservatism of the major parties in respect of governance system reforms is a major hurdle. Numerous Independent candidates make the effort to stand for Parliament but the electoral systems, especially for lower houses, are biased in favour of the major parties' establishment. These two parties now have very few members and are themselves lacking in adequate democratic organisation. Factional strife cannot be discounted. Clashes between Coalition partners will recur. Just recently, Australia witnessed a very public ugly stoush between the NSW Liberal Transport Minister Andrew Constance, candidate for a by-election in the marginal state seat of Eden-Monaro, a so-called bellwether seat, and another National Party candidate for that seat as well, John Barilaro. The ALP candidate Kirsten McBain may well have won the seat as a result!

Federally, the Senate presents a diversity of qualities that, for the moment, perhaps just manage to block most serious disasters from unfolding. The use of the Hare-Clark system of PR, although demonstrated as a flawed electoral system, even after being inadequately doctored in 2016, has fortunately prevented the worst effects of the SMD used for the House of Representatives.

With a few exceptions the media are part of the problem because while they sometimes do question the system, alternatives are generally not canvassed.

In particular, they basically refuse to discuss improvements to the system and its sub-systems. Virtually no media source inquired as to how it was even possible that a Government like that of Tony Abbott could be elected to power and, once elected, was kept in power for two years complete with a team of amateurs as Ministers. If this in itself is not a sign of dangerous flaws the election of five PMs in five years surely flags decline of grotesque proportions. Add to this the very low status of politicians in the public's rankings of occupations. Surely, it doesn't have to be like that. It should not be like that. Given that these people make major, far-reaching decisions for the country, this is a truly alarming situation. Australia has a large number of very well trained, capable people who are eminently qualified to head ministries but far too few of them are to be found in Parliaments.

The ARM should concern itself with such problems. Its objective should really be: ***What kind of Republic do we really want?*** Now is the time to do that. Having experienced a number of meetings with the ARM myself and several other pro-Republic groups in the noughties as the representative of the ***Republic Now*** group, the severe limitation of its very minimalist objective struck me as a major problem. Just changing the Head of State really does NOT make for a democratic Republic at all. And that is exactly what a Republic should be about: democracy. Why would the ARM advocate for a Republic that would automatically inherit such a lamentable political system? It could hardly be argued that a Republic with such a system is worth the name RESPUBLICA.

CONCLUSION

Many citizens no longer believe that Australia is a vibrant democracy that is run well, at least as far as the parliaments are concerned. They realise that the parliaments are only partly representative of the citizens; that they are often dominated by minorities. That staffers and private consultants with free access to their representatives play a major role in shaping legislation. That decentralisation is not happening. That the Indigenous issues are not solved, to the contrary. There is a growing awareness that there are serious governance problems and that they need to be fixed, despite improved approval ratings following the effective approach to the current health crisis. When the Coronavirus threat has been overcome, either fairly quickly, gradually or in some countries but not in others, at least two major governance issues will return: distrust in the political system and climate change. This book has primarily dealt with one, presenting the governance system as a vicious circle dominated by conservatism. But the Morrison Government also continues to have a major problem with accepting the science certainty about climate change. In January 2020 the PM even planned a Royal Commission on the subject. Most climate change scientists found this idea completely unnecessary. So, why delay proper action Mr. Morrison?

The National Cabinet will continue and COAG has been dissolved. This is a good move and could be the first step to dismantling of the federal system. It should take steps to develop a new electoral system and a new Constitution for Australia, including the issue of replacing the federal structure. If the need for system reform is more widely recognised alternatives can be canvassed, taught, and discussed in the media, especially by the public broadcasters. The ABC and SBS in particular could play a major role here and speed up the process as well. Public funding needs to be restored, to the ABC in particular. The universities and high schools need to address such developments much more actively than they have done in the past. The universities need to be concentrating on their traditional roles. They are not business corporations – and never should be. Political system renewal should be high on their teaching agendas.

Why is it that neither major party has been inclined to tackle governance system change? They pursue habitually, and predominantly, the class-oriented policies of yesteryear! The conservative Liberal Party/National Party Coalition vs the conservative Labor/ACTU, the "two sides of politics" as if there are no other significant political interests in this multicultural, diverse, middle-class society. Where are the reformers? We already read about the Coalition preparing for the post-Coronavirus period: economic recovery, meaning small government, lower taxes, trickle-down expectations, etc. From the more progressive quarters, like the left leaning *The Saturday Paper*, we read a recent editorial canvassing for a "Charter of Hope", a new attempt to create a Preamble to our archaic Constitution. However, this merely reflects just more piecemeal tinkering. There are major changes to be discussed and implemented. In economics we need to build on the country's natural and enduring strengths: 270 days of sunshine, grand gifts of nature to be admired by tourists from many countries, development of the extensive hospitality industries, the successful multiculturalist society, all industries that derive from and boost these natural advantages, like outstanding transport systems, new high tech industries, including electric cars.

However, amazingly Australia is now (April -August, 2020) witnessing an unprecedented period of cooperation in which these two parties are working together to combat a major health danger that may linger several more months, even years, as long as no vaccine is found to permanently contain the threat. In this period the parties and the society will have the opportunity to reflect on the political and constitutional future of the country more than ever before, an unexpected but real advantage. And many others, not members or supporters of these major parties, can get going as well. There are the numerous smaller parties, the Greens and several others, as well as plenty of Independents who can express their views on and advocacy of alternative systems.

They can start studying the advantages of proportional representation – party list. They can question the serious limitations of having to select Ministers ONLY from the elected representatives of just one major party.

Isn't it high time that we recruit the undoubted competencies of many people who would NOT want to have to ingratiate themselves with either of the major parties, or any other party, in order to be candidates for Ministerial appointment? Isn't this the time that we can question why we should continue with a Constitution so dated, reflecting predominantly the colonial values of the 1890s, progressive at the time no doubt, but constitutionally hardly changed since then.

Really, our democracy could be improved very substantially. This is the time to reflect AND to act on that realisation and opportunity.

REFERENCES

Books

Brett, Judith (2018) – *From secret ballot to democracy sausage,* Text Publishing, Melbourne.

Greenwood, Gordon (1946) – *The Future of Australian Federalism*, second edition, University of Queensland Press.

Hall, Rodney (1998) – *Abolish the States! Australia's Future and a $30 billion answer to our tax problems*, Pan MacMillan, Australia.

Harris, Bede (2012) – *Freedom, Democracy and Accountability – A Vision for a new Australian Constitution*, vivid Publishing

Harris, Bede (2014) – *Exploring the Frozen Continent, What Australians Think of Constitutional Reform*, Vivid Publishing.

Hil, Richard (2015) – *Why you won't get the university education you deserve -Selling Students Short*, Allen and Unwin.

Hennig, Brett (2017) – *The End of Politicians – Time for a Real Democracy,* Unbound

Hocking, Jenny (2008) – *Gough Whitlam –A Moment in History, Vol 1*, The Miegunyah Press.

Horne, Donald (1977) – *Change the Rules, Towards a Democratic Constitution*, Penguin.

Horne, Donald (1981) – *Winner Take All?* Penguin

Horne, Donald (1992) – *The coming Republic*, Pan MacMillan.

Levy, Ron, O'Brien, Molly, Rice, Simon, Ridge, Pauline & Thornton, Margaret (eds) (2017) – *New Directions for Law in Australia – Essays in Contemporary Law Reform*, ANU, Canberra.

Lijphart, Arend (2012) – *Patterns of Democracy: Government Forms and Performance in Thirty-six countries*, Second edition, Yale University Press, New Haven

Patmore, G. & Jungwirth, G. (2002) – *Labour Essays entitled The Big Makeover – a new Australian Constitution*, Pluto Press.

Rivkin, Jeremy (2019) – *The Green New Deal*, St. Martin's Press, NY.

Robertson, Geoffrey (2013) – *Dreaming too loud- Reflections on a Race Apart*, Vintage books

Rugg, Sally (2019) – *How powerful we are – Behind the scenes with of Australia's leading activists*, Hachette, Australia

Semler, Ricardo (1993) – *Maverick, the success story behind the world's most unusual workplace*, Arrow – Random House

Turnbull, Malcolm (2020) – *A Bigger Picture*, Hardie Grant Books

Walsh, Richard (2017) – *Reboot – Democracy make-over to empower Australian voters,* MUP.

Woldring, Klaas (2018) – *YES, we can........rewrite the Australian Constitution,* BookPod, Melbourne.

Woldring, K., Nicholas, A., Snow, J. and Drummond, M (eds) (2014) – *Beyond Federation – Options to renew Australia's 1901 Constitution*, BookPod/ Amazon.

Woldring. K. (2006) – *How about OUR Republic?* BookPod, Melbourne

Articles, reports, research/conference papers, URL pieces, etc.

ABC program "Difference Opinion", 30.8.2007. Participants Prof. Ann Twomey, Vice Chancellor Greg Craven, Dr. Margaret Kelly and A/Prof. Klaas Woldring

ACTU/TDC – *Australia Reconstructed Report*, 1987

Anthony, K. – *The Political Representation of Ethnic and Racial Minorities*, NSW, Parliamentary Research Paper, 2006

Appleby, Gabrielle – *The High Court sticks to the letter of the law on the citizenship seven,* The Conversation, 27 October 2017 available online: https://theconversation.com/the-high-court-sticks-to-the-letter-of-the-law-on-thecitizenship-seven-85324.

Australian Law Reform Commission – *The Future of Law Reform: A Suggested Program of Work 2020-25,* Australian Government, 2019

Bankwest Curtin Economics Centre – *Finding a Place to Call Home*. Perth, BCEC, 2019

Brett, Judith – *"The Coal Curse -- Resources, Climate and Australia's Future",* Quarterly Essay, Issue 78 2020.

Chifley Research Centre (2019) – *"Towards 2022 – Ideas for Labor and Australia"*

Cooke, Richard – *"Descent from the Summit – Looking back on Kevin Rudd's 2020 vision"*, The Monthly, March 2020

Davis, Megan – *No time for the meek – Keeping faith with the Uluru reforms*, The Monthly, October 2019

Dutch Workplace Relation Act – https://www.worker-participation.eu/National-Industrial-Relations/Countries/Netherlands/Workplace-Representation

Evans, M., Halupka, M and Stoker, G. – Trust and Democracy in Australia, Institute for Governance and Policy Analysis, Canberra University, 2018 http://www.hpw.org.au/uploads/5/9/1/7/59177601/boedker_vidgen_meagher_cogin_mouritsen_and_runnalls_2011_high_performing_workplaces_index_october_6_2011.pdf

Ireland, Judith – *Backstage in Canberra: Who is lobbying our MPs?* SMH, 1.10.2019

Lambert, Scott – *Not fit for purpose – re-imagining the Australian Constitution,* The Mandarin. https://www.themandarin.com.au/86092-not-fit-purpose-reimagining-australian-constitution/#.Wh3So2xa-fE.email.

Leading for Change (2018) – https://www.humanrights.gov.au/our-work/race-discrimination/publications/leading-change-blueprint-cultural-diversity-and-0

Megalogenis, George – *The Middle of Nowhere*, The Monthly, Summer Edition December 2019/January 2020

Megalogenis, George – *Australasia Rising*, Good Weekend, 25. January 2019

Muller, Damien – *"The new Senate Voting system and the 2016 election"*, Parliamentary Library, Canberra 25.1.2018

Patience, Allan – https://johnmenadue.com/allan-patience-the-coronavirus-pandemic-and-the-crisis-of-australian-federalism/

Report of the Royal Commission on the Electoral System in New Zealand, December 1986.

Slattery, Luke – *Silver tail subversives: the men aiming to change a system in which they prosper* SMH's Good Weekend, 23.6.2016

Taub, Amanda – https://www.nytimes.com/2019/12/16/world/europe/uk-election-brexit.html

Uhr, John – *"Why we Chose Proportional Representation"* in Sawer, Marian & Miskin, Sarah (1999) *"Representation and Institutional change – 50 years of Proportional representation in the Senate"*, ANU & Department of

the Senate, Canberra. https://www.aph.gov.au/senate/~/~/link.aspx?_
id=DB8FD989ADD34452AF9F0792790FF7DF

Woldring, Klaas – *Why the Australian people must rewrite their entire Constitution*, Annual Conference Australian Political Science Conference, 1992 Canberra (abridged version – published in APSA Newsletter, No. 66, September 1993)

Woldring, Klaas & Van den Akker, Jose – *Multiculturalism is a strength in rebounding from COVID-19 crisis,* Independent Australia, 3 May 2020

www.ingramcontent.com/pod-product-compliance
Lightning Source LLC
Chambersburg PA
CBHW070813290326
41931CB00011BB/2206